GW00975930

Canary Islands

- A in the text denotes a highly recommended sight
- A complete A–Z of practical information starts on p.104
- Extensive mapping throughout: on cover flaps and in text

Berlitz Publishing Company, Inc.

Princeton   Mexico City   Dublin   Eschborn   Singapore

Text:	Paul Murphy
Photography:	Paul Murphy
Staff Editor	Jane Middleton
Cartography:	🌐 Falk-Verlag, Munich
Layout:	Media Content Marketing, Inc.

Although the publisher tries to insure the accuracy of all the information in this book, changes are inevitable and errors may result. The publisher cannot be responsible for any resulting loss, inconvenience, or injury. If you find an error in this guide, please let the editors know by writing to Berlitz Publishing Company, 400 Alexander Park, Princeton, NJ 08540-6306.

ISBN 2-8315-6293-7
Revised 1997 – Third Printing April 1999

Printed in Switzerland by Weber SA, Bienne
039/904 RP

CONTENTS

The Islands and the People	7

A Brief History	10

Where to Go	19
Tenerife	19
Gran Canaria	34
Lanzarote	47
Fuerteventura	56
Gomera	61
La Palma	66
El Hierro	70

What to Do	73
Sports	73
Other Activities	78
For Children	83
Shopping	85
Nightlife	89

Eating Out	**91**
Index	**101**
Handy Travel Tips	**104**
Hotels and Restaurants	**129**

Maps

Las Palmas de Gran Canaria	38
La Palma	67
El Hierro	70

CANARY ISLANDS

THE ISLANDS
AND THE PEOPLE

The Canary Islands are seven specks of rock, scattered over 300 miles in the middle of the vast Atlantic Ocean. To the east lies the Sahara, from where the beaches of Fuerteventura have blown; to the northeast lies the North of Africa, from where the Guanches — the original Canarians — once came. And to the north lies Spain, from where Conquistadors, colonialists, and latter-day lawmakers have laid the foundations for modern Canaries life.

From farther north still come new Conquistadors wearing shorts and sunglasses. English, German, and Scandinavian hordes are now descending on the islands all year round. Their effect on the Canaries is good for the tourism business but hasn't always been so good for the environment. However, while certain areas, notably the southern coasts of Gran Canaria and Tenerife, have capitalized on tourism and capitulated on the wider issues, newcomers to tourism, such as Lanzarote, are progressing more slowly and surely. The smaller islands have yet to make up their minds, but as they all lack commercially exploitable beaches it seems unlikely that they will be experiencing more than a comparative handful of visitors in the near future. And overall, if all the land devoted to tourism was to be added up, it would still occupy only a mere fraction of the islands' total area and natural wealth.

The diversity of landscapes on the islands is quite amazing. While Fuerteventura is truly a desert island — windswept, sandy, and bare — La Palma is lush, verdant, and fertile. And if the strikingly beautiful interiors of Tenerife, Gran Canaria, and Gomera are Gardens of Eden then the stark *malpaís* (badlands) of Lanzarote are surely the Valleys of Hell. The Canaries are volcanic islands, and volcanic is-

Canary-style holiday apartments in Puerto de la Cruz.

lands are never dull. La Palma erupted as recently as 1971. On Lanzarote you can not only gaze at the awesome scenery created by earth-shattering events that occurred centuries ago, you can also watch your lunch cooking now over the heat of the volcano beneath your feet.

What of the people themselves? Canarians look Spanish, speak Spanish, are imbued with Spanish culture, and to all intents and purposes are little different from their mainland cousins. They work hard, enjoy their food, siesta, and fiestas, and know how to turn a tourist dollar.

So which is the best island for you? It may be a cliché but it is nonetheless true that there is an island for every kind of person.

Tenerife is the biggest island in almost every sense. In Mount Teide it features the biggest scenery and it certainly has the greatest number of tourist attractions by day and night. In terms of all-round appeal, however, Gran Canaria runs a close second. Both have bustling new cities and sleepy old towns to visit, both have wonderful inland scenery and charming villages to explore, and both have modern resorts ranging from good-time to quiet-time. If a long stretch of golden beach is a priority then Gran Canaria has the edge.

Lanzarote will delight all those people who are environmentally aware yet enjoy the company of other tourists. Whether or not the island can solve this paradox of modern tourism is yet to be seen, but the tourist attractions masterminded by design guru César Manrique and the general ambience of this low-rise island are very appealing.

Fuerteventura tends to polarize opinion: Is it an oasis in the middle of an overcomplicated world, as some have claimed, or is it simply the desert of first impression? The beaches here are certainly the best in the Canaries, and resorts to suit most tastes are springing up. Watersports aside, though, there isn't much else to do or see, which may be fine as long as you know in advance.

The lesser-known islands of Gomera, El Hierro, and La Palma are for the hardier, more inquisitive travellers. There are relatively few comfortable hotels, no international restaurants, and — best of all, as far as many are concerned — almost no tourists. If you enjoy walking through beautiful mountain scenery for days on end, if you don't mind conversing with the aid of a phrase book in the local village bar, and your idea of nightlife is gazing at the North Star, then one of these islands may be your Shangri-La. For most people, though, a day or two away from it all is enough. Island-hopping is relatively easy and a few days on an unspoiled island combined with the creature comforts of a major resort offer the best of both worlds. Travel independently, look around the corner from the next hotel, and you will soon discover that there is much more to the Canaries than just another winter sun tan.

A BRIEF HISTORY

As the clouds cascade down the hillside to reveal the magical summit of Mount Teide, or the sun rises above the eerie moonscape of Lanzarote's Montañas del Fuego, even the most cynical onlooker will realize that the Canaries are a land of legends. The ancient Greeks and Romans called this archipelago the Fortunate Islands, and Homer tells us that blessed ones were sent to the Elysian Fields to enjoy eternal happiness in a land where winter was unknown. Could this have been the Canaries?

The author Plutarch wrote of fertile lands somewhere off the coast of Africa, where the breezes of springtime never stop. His source was the Roman leader Sertorius, who had heard of the lands from an explorer.

Many writers link the lost continent of Atlantis with the Canaries. According to Plato, this rich, happy land, lying somewhere to the west of Gibraltar in the Atlantic Ocean, was destroyed by earthquakes and tidal waves nearly 12,000 years ago. After the cataclysm only the mountain tops of Atlantis remained above the sea and constituted seven islands. The Canaries perhaps?

From Plato to Jules Verne the possibilities have stirred people's imagination, ranging from the theories of learned academics to the ramblings of wild eccentrics. By now the truth is surely lost in the myths and mists of time. What is undeniable, however, is the magical presence that these seven volcanic sisters possess. When you sight Mount Teide on a distant horizon you will understand the profusion of legends.

The barren beauty of Los Roques.

The First Inhabitants

Long before the first European sailors beached in the Canaries, all seven islands were inhabited. These original Canarians came to be termed Guanches, meaning in the native tongue "man" (strictly speaking this name applies only to the original inhabitants of Tenerife).

The Guanches are thought to have arrived in the islands around the 1st or 2nd century B.C., probably from North Africa. Ethnographers link them with the Cro-Magnon period. They were tall, white-skinned, often blue-eyed and blond-haired. You can see their remains in the meticulous collection of the Museo Canario in Las Palmas on Gran Canaria. Here too you can study their preoccupation with death. Like the ancient Egyptians they carefully embalmed their dead, presumably for a ceremonial passage to the next world. Cryptic rock carvings have been found which may explain these rituals, but so far no one has found the Canarian version of the Rosetta Stone with which to decipher them.

Columbus was here too. A fine bust in Vegueta, Las Palmas, on Gran Canaria.

Another baffling mystery is how the Guanches arrived on the islands. No evidence of Guanche boats has ever been discovered, so were they marooned here by pirates or perhaps exiled by their own people? One theory is that they may have floated across from North Africa on reed craft. The expeditions of Thor Heyerdahl do lend some credence to this idea.

In keeping with their Berber origins the Guanches were cave dwellers, though by no means all Guanches lived in the rocks and many of the original caves that remain today (for example the Cuevas de Valerón on Gran Canaria) were probably used only for storage. Cave dwelling in such a climate is a logical idea, being cooler in summer and warmer in winter than more conventional accommodation. Even today there are many cave dwellings in the islands.

A Guanche legacy that you will see at the market place and in traditional eating houses is *gofio*, a finely ground toasted flour that is still a traditional Canarian staple. The Guanche language also lives on in place names such as Tafira and Tamadaba (on Gran Canaria), Timanfaya (on Lanzarote), Teide (on Tenerife), and Tenerife itself.

Conquistadors

The first foreign visitors to the Canaries are thought to have been Arab sailors who landed on Gran Canaria some 2,000 years ago and were met warmly. In later centuries the islanders' gracious hospitality was to cost them dearly.

Europeans did not arrive until the 14th century, when the Genoese sailor Lanzarotto Marcello colonized the island, known then in native tongue as Tytheroygatra and subsequently as Lanzarote. Slave traders, treasure seekers, and missionaries all followed in Lanzarotto's wake, but it was not until 1402 that the European conquest of the Canaries began in earnest. At its helm was the Norman baron, Jean de Béthencourt, under service to Henry III, king of Castile.

After the baron had taken Lanzarote and Fuerteventura with comparative ease, his ships were scattered by storm off Gran Canaria. He next turned to El Hierro, where the awestruck islanders welcomed the new visitors arriving in their great floating vessels as gods. Béthencourt returned the hospitality by inviting the natives aboard his ships. He took them captive and sold them into slavery.

Around this time the Portuguese, who had also been colonizing the Atlantic, turned their attention to the Canaries. Naval skirmishes ensued between the two powers, but at the end of the war of succession between Portugal and Castile, the wide-ranging Treaty of Alcaçovas ended Lisbon's claims to the Fortunate Islands.

By order of Ferdinand and Isabella of Castile, the second phase of the conquest was set in motion. By 1483 Gran Canaria had been subdued and in 1488 Gomera was taken. La Palma held out until 1493, and after another two years of furious fighting the biggest prize of all, Tenerife, was in Spanish hands. The process of pacification and conversion to the Christian faith had taken almost a century of bloody guerilla warfare with thousands of casualties, sustained mainly on the brave but ill-equipped Guanche side.

The World Is Round!

Just as the conquest of the Canaries was reaching its climax, Christopher Columbus (Cristobal Colón in Spanish) was planning his historic expedition in search of a sea route to the East Indies. Each of the Canaries boasts some connection with Columbus, who came to the islands because they were then the world's most westerly charted points and therefore the last stopping point before venturing into the unknown.

The great navigator definitely stopped off at Gomera and Las Palmas on his voyage of 1492 and he even recorded a

Scenic tilling — farmers work the fields by hand, maintaining harmony with the environment on Lanzarote.

volcanic eruption while passing Tenerife. Not surprisingly his crew took this as an ill omen but, as history tells us, once past El Hierro they did not drop off the edge of the world after all. Columbus's routes and Canarian connections may be traced at the atmospheric Casa de Colón in Las Palmas (see page 38).

The role of the islands as a bridge between the Old World and the New World has continued down the centuries. Canarians have settled in Latin America in large numbers, usually in search of a better way of life, and news from Venezuela and Cuba is treated almost as a local item in the

Canary Islands newspapers. Canarian bananas provided the stock for those of the Caribbean, and in spoken accent and musical rhythms the Canaries lie halfway between Spain and South America.

Wine and Warfare

The Canaries' first major agricultural enterprise was sugar. Sugar canes sprouted easily on the islands, and during the first half of the 16th century a burgeoning industry developed. Boom turned to bust, however, with cheaper sugar production from Brazil and the Antilles and the industry died.

Still, trade links had at least been established with both the Old and the New World, and wine became the new farming venture to bolster the economy. Grapes grown in the volcanic soil produced a distinctive, full-bodied malmsey wine *(malvasía)* that became the fashionable drink of aristocratic Europe. Shakespeare and Voltaire, among others, were lavish in their praise, and today's island visitors can still sample the excellent wine in *bodegas*, restaurants, or even from the *supermercado*. When touring the islands you may still see old disused wine presses *(lagares)* on hillsides.

By the end of the 18th century the Canaries were a sufficiently important trading point to attract all types of pirates. In 1797 Horatio Nelson attacked Santa Cruz de Tenerife in search of a Spanish treasure ship. The defenders responded vigorously, accounting for the lives of 226 British sailors and the removal of the lower part of Nelson's saluting arm. The Santa Cruzeros clearly had no hard feelings towards the Admiral, however. Once it was known that the attack had been repelled, a gift of wine was sent out to Nelson (England was, after all, an important wine market) and a street was named Calle de Horacio Nelson in his honour!

Free Trade

By the early 18th century Canarians had become fully Spanish in both outlook and loyalties, and many volunteers joined the Peninsular War (Spaniards call it the War of Independence) which ended in 1814 with the restoration of Ferdinand VII to the Spanish throne.

Economic problems arose in the early 19th century, and the wine industry started to fail. Luckily another single-crop opportunity presented itself in the form of cochineal, a parasitic insect attracted to the *opuntia* variety of cactus. The tiny bodies of the female bugs contain a dark-red liquid perfect for dyeing, and for 50 years or so, millions of bugs were crushed for the sake of the Canarian economic good.

The Bug Bubble burst with the rise of chemical dyes in the 1870s. With the failure of yet another mono-culture, the Spanish government felt constrained to help the Canarian economy. In the mid-19th century free port status was granted by royal decree to one port in each of the islands (two in Tenerife). The lowering of duties and trade barriers at a time of considerable shipping expansion had the desired effect, and Santa Cruz de Tenerife and Las Palmas soon became two of the world's busiest ports.

The most recent major crop to come from the Canaries is bananas. The variety is dwarf banana, small and very tasty, and today demand actually outstrips production in some areas. The first exports were made in the 1880s and the banana has continued to be a mainstay of the islands' economy. Despite some recent problems and concern for the future, it is hoped that bananas will continue to be an important Canarian crop alongside their other staples, tomatoes and potatoes.

The Spanish Civil War

The plot that sparked off the Spanish Civil War was hatched in the Canary Islands. In 1936 a group of senior officers, discontented with the policies of the Spanish Republican Government, met in secret in the woods of La Esperanza on Tenerife. They had come to meet a fellow officer, Francisco Franco, whom the government had banished to the Canaries for subversive plotting. From the Canaries Franco took off for North Africa, the launching pad for the insurgent right-wing attack.

Three years later his armies had triumphed in a ruthless struggle that cost hundreds of thousands of Spanish lives. The Canaries were not spared the horrors of the war (mass Republican executions took place in the aptly named Barranco del Infierno, the Gorge of Hell, on Tenerife), but on the whole the islands prospered during Franco's period of dictatorship, which gave added protection to their free-port status.

Tourism

The massive growth of tourism in the islands since the 1960s has in some cases literally refaced the landscape, with brand-new resorts such as Playa de las Américas springing up like Gold Rush boom towns. However, such developments are mostly the exception and whole swathes of even the more developed islands are virtually untouched, while Gomera, El Hierro, and La Palma are only now starting to provide even the most basic tourist facilities. The infrastructure and transport system of the islands have meanwhile improved drastically, and since 1978 regional autonomy has provided the islanders with their long-desired break with Madrid (though they are still linked to some extent).

WHERE TO GO

In this section we examine each of the islands individually, its geography and personality, where to stay, and what to see.

TENERIFE
Area: 2,046 square km (790 square miles)
Population: 611,000

Tenerife is not only the largest of the Canaries geographically, it also offers the tourist more sights, more attractions, more towns and cities to explore, and more contrasts than any of the other islands. Where else in the Atlantic can you look round a banana plantation then take a short drive half way up a mountain for a snowball fight?

The mountain in question is Teide (it rhymes with lady), at 3,718 meters (12,198 feet) the tallest in all Spain. The symbol of the island, it can be seen from vantage points all over Tenerife, but for the very best views you too need to be high above its ring of clouds.

Tenerife has been welcoming visitors from cold northern climes since the 19th century. However, the focus has changed from the cloudy, green north coast where Puerto de la Cruz was once the favourite resort (it is still enormously popular) to the hot, dry, arid south. By day the beaches are packed with glistening bodies; by night the streets throb to a new sort of holidaymaker's beat, far removed from the travellers who used to visit the island on doctor's orders.

Santa Cruz de Tenerife

The capital of Tenerife (population 220,000) and the administrative centre for the westerly Canaries, Santa Cruz is not a city in which tourists spend a great deal of time. This is a pity, because although there are few tourist attractions and it

Local produce at the Mercado de Nuestra Señora:
spicy dried peppers .

is not especially beautiful, the city possesses an undeniably authentic Spanish charm, proud of its colonial heritage, but with its feet planted solidly in the real world.

Until the advent of the air-package holiday, most visitors to Tenerife disembarked at Santa Cruz by the long, well-kept maritime promenade, and this is still the best starting point for exploring the city. The hub is the **Plaza de España,** in the middle of which stands a four-sided cross, a memorial to the dead of the Spanish Civil War. The huge, drab, grey building adjacent to the Plaza is the Cabildo Insular (local government headquarters) which also houses the tourist office and the **Museo Arqueológico,** with important exhibits illustrating the life and death rituals of Guanche society (see page 12).

The city's other museum of note is the **Museo Municipal de Bellas Artes,** which lies on Calle José Murphy and includes some fine Spanish and Flemish works. The adjacent church of San Francisco is also worth a visit.

The area extending up the hill from the plaza is the island's banking centre. On the Plaza de la Candelaria one bank is housed in the beautiful **Palacio de Carta** building, which dates from 1742. The main shopping area continues along Calle del Castillo; the parallel street, Calle Béthencourt Alfonso, is also a major avenue. For craft shops visit Artespaña on Plaza de la Candelaria. The most vibrant shopping area is a short walk away at the **Mercado de Nuestra Señora de Africa**. This clean, airy, modern area is full of small competing stalls, selling all manner of fresh meat, fish, fruit, vegetables, and flowers. On Saturdays colourful flowers are everywhere, and on Sundays the adjacent *rastro* (flea market) is the big attraction.

The bridge to the Mercado crosses a *barranco* (ravine) where goats graze, oblivious to all the activity. Follow the *barranco* to the seafront to discover the **Iglesia Matriz de la Concepción** (Church of the Immaculate Conception). Dating from the early 16th century, this is the town's most important historical building and contains several interesting relics, including Nelson's faded battle flag (see page 16). A notice on the door tells you where the key is held, should you wish to look inside.

One of the most charming aspects of the city is its picturesque squares and gardens. Situated conveniently for shoppers at the very end of Calle del Castillo is the flower-decked square of **Plaza del General Weyler**, a perfect spot for a drink and a snack. If you are interested in ceramics, walk a short way along Avenida 25 de Julio to the Plaza of the same name to admire the delightful tiled benches here. Many are adorned with colourful ceramic advertising messages from the 1920s. The city's finest park, **Parque García Sanabria**, is a few yards along the same street. Cool and shady on a hot day, it is famous for its fountains and its floral clock. The park borders the **Rambla del General Franco**, the city's most splendid avenue, brightened by leafy trees and elegant houses that are reminders of both past and present glories.

Follow the coast road for 9 km (5½ miles) and you will find the best beach on the island, incongruously located just past the oil terminal. **Las Teresitas** is a beautiful golden crescent of Saharan sand stretching almost a mile and measuring some 91 meters (300 feet) wide. A few *kioscos* selling paella and tortillas are the only beachside developments, while the adjacent small fishing port of San Andrés lends local colour. A breakwater parallel to the shoreline keeps the sand in and the water clean, and provides perfectly safe family swimming. Las Teresitas is often crowded with Santa Cruceros in summer, but in winter it is rarely busy.

Puerto de la Cruz

Puerto, as this town of 28,000 is often abbreviated to, has neither good beaches nor the abundant sunshine of the south, yet for many travellers it is the most complete resort on the island. Like Santa Cruz it has been attracting convalescing northern Europeans for over a century and it maintains much of its colonial grandeur. The seafront promenade, from the surfing beach of Playa de Martiánez along to the **Puerto Pesquero** (the old fishing port), has been quite heavily commercialized but not at all spoiled, and the atmosphere is always lively without being boisterous.

The problem of Puerto's lack of a decent beach was brilliantly addressed by the late César Manrique, who designed **Lago Martiánez**. This 3 hectare (8 acre) complex of tropical lagoons, cascading fountains and sunbathing terraces is cleverly landscaped with lush palms and black and white vol-

The beachfront development of Puerto's Lago Martiánez has Mount Teide as a backdrop.

canic rockery to fit perfectly into the seafront, where the surf crashes spectacularly against the rocks. Adjacent is the popular meeting point of the Café Colombus, where you can catch free buses to various attractions.

The charming pedestrianized street of **Calle de San Telmo** descends into town, passing the delightful tiny white 18th-century Ermita de San Telmo. A little farther on is the majestic 17th-century **Iglesia de la Peña de Francia** (Church of the Rock of France), definitely worth a look inside.

The main square, **Plaza de Charco**, is the hub of both tourist and local life, and its numerous cafés, restaurants, and shops are busy at all hours. Just off the square, the old town around the Puerto Pesquero is remarkably oblivious to change. Among the narrow streets with faded wooden balconies and carved doors are the **Casa de Miranda**, now a crafts shop and restaurant, and, oldest of all, the **Casa de la Real Aduana** (Customs House), facing the tiny port and built in 1620. More ancient Canarian architecture can be found on Calle Iriarte (off Calle Blanco), including the **Casa Iriarte**, a crafts shop, and naval museum.

The major tourist attractions lie just outside town. The biggest is **Loro Parque**, which houses the world's largest collection of parrots — more than 230 species in beautiful subtropical gardens. Other amusements include performing dolphins, a cinema with a 180-degree screen, a performing parrot show, flamingos, and a walk-through aquarium with sharks, giant octopus, and a huge variety of fish. The oldest attraction is undoubtedly the **Jardín Botánico** (Botanical Garden), founded by royal decree in 1788 and located on the road to La Orotava. This dense jungle covers some 2.5 hectares (6 acres). There are palms of every variety and the centrepiece is a huge South American fig tree whose enormous branches and roots have become intertwined into one great tree house.

On the same road (and everywhere on the island the roadsides are fragrant with honeysuckle and mimosa and they blush with bougainvillaea and jacaranda) is **Bananera El Guanche**, a working plantation open to the public every day. This provides a fascinating insight into how a Canarian banana plantation operates. It also boasts a superb collection of exotic trees, shrubs, flowers, and cacti from all over the world. Browse awhile in their shop for botanical and other gifts.

High above the centre of town stands the landmark **Casino Taoro**, floodlit by night. This is your chance to spin the roulette wheel, play a hand of blackjack, or pull on the slot machine handle. A much cheaper option is simply to observe the assorted tourists and local big spenders at play.

Points North

La Laguna is Tenerife's second largest town and is known as the ecclesiastic and cultural capital of the island. Here you can escape fellow tourists almost completely, if you wish. Walk through street after narrow street of distinguished old houses; sometimes a door left ajar will reveal a Moorish-style Canaries patio, rich with plants, brightly tiled, perhaps even with a fountain — a refuge of cool, green tranquillity.

Start at the **Plaza del Adelantado**, which is home to several beautiful buildings, including the Palacio de Nava and the convent of Santa Catalina, both dating from the 17th century. A short way along Calle Obispo Rey Redondo is the **cathedral** of La Laguna with its landmark twin bell towers. It is a surprisingly modern structure in spite of its design, consecrated in 1913, over 400 years after the city was founded. Go inside to admire its huge vaulted ceiling, ornate fittings, and the 16th-century Flemish altar panels.

> When visiting churches, shorts, backless dresses, and tank tops should not be worn.

Continue on the same street to the town's oldest church, **Iglesia de Nuestra Señora de la Concepción** (Church of the Immaculate Conception), built in 1497. Its seven-story belfry and watchtower were added two centuries later. The interior is outstanding, with exquisite timber carvings on the ceiling, and pulpit and an enormous baroque altarpiece with Flemish panels. Despite its wealth of tradition, La Laguna is a surprisingly youthful city, boasting the only full-scale university in the archipelago.

Tacoronte is famous locally for its wine, and a good place to check this out is at the Bodegas Alfaro. The town is also renowned for a much-venerated 17th-century figure of Christ. Known as the **Cristo de los Dolores** (Christ of Sorrows) it stands in the local church of the same name. There is also the beautiful 16th-century Iglesia de Santa Catalina to visit. North of the town at Valle Guerra is the Casa de Carta Museum of Ethnography.

Bajamar is a growing tourist centre and, like Puerto de la Cruz, has cleverly compensated for its lack of beachfront. When the sea comes in it is corralled into large artificial pools. At high tide the waves surge in, ensuring a constantly changing supply of water. The Anaga mountains provide a fine backdrop to the town.

After passing the semi-tropical plateau around La Laguna, the road going northeast begins to climb into a zone of remarkably lush vegetation. The forest of **Monte de las Mercedes** is a cool, dark world of towering laurels, beech, pine, and wildflowers. At the end of a serpentine road there is a dizzying view from the 960-meter- (3,149-foot-) high *mirador* (lookout point) of **Pico del Inglés**. Look due north towards Punta del Hidalgo with its churning seas then turn to face south towards the golden sands of Las Teresitas. Northeast of the *mirador,* the picturesque village of **Taganana** is worth the detour to see the church's 16th-century triptych showing the nativity, adoration of the Magi, and circumcision of Christ.

The Central Area

La Orotava is a remarkably well-preserved, unspoiled old town set on a steep hill high above Puerto de la Cruz. Stately mansions, ancient churches, and cobbled streets are its trademarks. The twin towers, baroque facade, and Byzantine dome of the **Iglesia Nuestra Señora de la Concepción** dominate a fascinating skyline which has remained virtually unchanged for centuries. The present church dates from 1788 and features a marble and alabaster high altar, priceless gold and silver treasures, and important sculptures.

Walk on up the steep hill passing (to the left) the Palacio Municipal and the Jardín Botánico. Continue on up to Calle San Francisco and the **Casas de los Balcones** (Houses of the Balconies). The balconies in question are inside the house's courtyard and are some of the finest examples of their kind. This splendid 17th-century mansion and the Casa de Turista (1590) opposite are now shops dedicated to Canary handicrafts. Here you can see girls in traditional costume embroidering and lace-making and you may also see craftsmen demonstrating the "pavement art" for which the town is famous. The upper floors of the Casas de los Balcones, previously the private living quarters of a wealthy family, have recently been opened to the public as a museum, and are well worth seeing.

Continue up Calle San Francisco to the 18th-century **Hospital de la Santísima Trinidad** (Hospital of the Holy Trinity). The revolving drum on the hospital door was once used as an anonymous delivery box for unwanted babies. The hospital terrace offers a fine view of the **Orotava Valley**, some 62 square km (24 square miles) of greenery with flaming bushes and bright blue flowers. On seeing this valley for the first time, the German naturalist Alexander Von Humboldt is said to have fallen to his knees to thank God for such a marvel of creation. Today, sadly, much of it has been obliterated by housing developments.

Painting by Sand

To celebrate the feast of Corpus Christi in May and June, detailed works of art are made by spreading multi-coloured volcanic rock and sand particles on the ground in the same way that a conventional artist would spread paint onto a canvas. The Plaza Franco in front of the Palacio Municipal is the site for one such large-scale ground stone artwork. Similar pictures are created with flowers both here and at La Laguna (see Festivals page 78).

Von Humboldt is commemorated at the Mirador Humboldt, halfway between La Orotava and Santa Ursula, close to the motorway. Santa Ursula is a pleasant small town known locally for its many fine eating places. Just north of here are the two small towns of La Matanza and La Victoria de Acentejo, more notable for their historical significance than their present-day attractions.

There are several approaches to **Las Cañadas National Park** and **Mount Teide**. The park is well signposted from the motorway via La Orotava, but if you are coming from the north then the most picturesque route is via **La Esperanza**. The small town soon gives way to a lush forest of giant pines and eucalyptus trees. Four km (2½ miles) south at Las Raíces is where Franco met with his co-conspirators in 1936 (see page 18). An obelisk in the forest commemorates the event. As the road gains altitude and temperatures fall, the views become ever more spectacular. The Mirador Pico de las Flores looks out over to the southeast and the Mirador de Ortuño offers a panorama of the northern coast. Highest of all at over 2,000 meters (6,562 feet) **Mirador las Cumbres** reveals Teide in all her glory.

The entrance to the National Park is **El Portillo de las Cañadas**, where there is a visitor centre and a small exhibition area. If you wish to walk in the park, pick up a leaflet or ask for information about the daily guided walks. Note that during winter the environment can become quite harsh, and you should never undertake winter walks without consulting staff at the visitor centre first. At this point it is quite likely that you will be in the clouds, temperatures are very low, and in winter there may well be snow on the ground.

Casa de los Balcones. Sympathically converted to a shop and museum.

The landscape is becoming very lunar-like; it was around here that some of the filming for *Planet of the Apes* took place.

As you continue ever upwards you will eventually drive through the clouds and bright warm sunshine will greet you again. The ascent to the top of Mount Teide can be made by cable car (*teleférico*) or by climbing. Most visitors choose the cable car, but it's worth noting that in summer the queues are very long and even after leaving the cable car it is still a climb of another 160 meters (525 feet) to the summit, 3,717 meters (12,195 feet). Once at the top you should be able to count off all the other Canary Islands and, on a good day, see North Africa. Sulphurous fumes will remind you that a volcano is beneath your feet. Don't worry — it has been dormant since the end of the 17th century.

Impressive as Teide is, it is basically no more than a peak on the edge of a giant volcano which long ago erupted or imploded to leave behind the vast Caldera (volcanic crater) which is most apparent from the area known as **Los Roques**. Los Roques are a group of giant, flamboyantly shaped lumps of volcanic rock rising out of the crater, much visited, and much photographed. The *parador* here is a good place (and indeed the only place) for refreshments.

The East and South Coast

Candelaria is a town with deep religious roots. Legend has it that well before Christianity came to the Canaries an image of the Virgin was washed ashore here and worshipped by the Guanches, who were quite oblivious to its significance. The Spaniards later built a church dedicated to the statue. Sadly both the statue and the church were destroyed in 1826 when a tidal wave reclaimed the Virgin. The present over-sized **basilica** was built soon afterwards.

The splendid new statue of Nuestra Señora de la Candelaria, the patron saint of the Canary Islands, is the object of a major pilgrimage in mid August. This helps to explain the large number of refreshment places and the huge basilica plaza, which outside of pilgrimage times looks rather bare. The Guanches are not forgotten either: ten chieftains stand guard in a row, with their backs to the Atlantic. These idealized cavemen are truly noble savages.

There is little of interest south of Candelaria until Reina Sofía Airport. Directly south of the airport is the charming fishing village of **El Abrigo**, where fine fish restaurants line the seafront. Its popularity means that a meal with a view can be quite expensive, so it's worth checking the price before you order. The coast west of here is known as La Costa del Silencio (the Silent Coast). This rugged (some might say desolate) shoreline is punctuated by developments at the fishing port of Las Galletas and the attractive *urbanización* of Ten-Bel. This is also a good area for golfers, since the 18-hole championship courses of Amarilla Golf and Country Club and Golf del Sur are nearby.

The most popular tourist destinations in Tenerife are the adjacent resorts of **Los Cristianos** and **Playa de Las Américas**. Los Cristianos used to be a small fishing port with a quiet little beach. It now plays host to hundreds of thousands of mainly British and German holidaymakers each year and

---

What's In A Name?

La Matanza, "the massacre," refers to a bloody Guanche victory at this site in 1494, when 900 Spanish troops were ambushed in a deep ravine. A year and a half later at nearby Acentejo the Spanish exacted their revenge with interest, killing some 2,000 Guanches. *Victoria* (victory) was proclaimed and a chapel built in celebration. Within a few months the century-old Canaries campaign was over.

its small beach is woefully inadequate. Traces of the old town can still be found around the port, though it is difficult to locate anything but British or German bars and restaurants along the crowded beach front. The fishing boats here do at least add some local colour, and all sorts of excursions can be booked: deep-sea fishing for shark and swordfish, piratical expeditions aboard a fully rigged tallship, or a **boat safari** in search of pilot whales and dolphins.

Playa de las Américas was born in the 1970s and has quickly developed from a bare shoreline to the high-rise, high-energy, highly packaged resort it is today. Here the beachside bars are not Spanish, nor even international: they are either German or English. If your idea of a holiday is to mix solely with people of your own nationality and to avoid "foreign food" ("No Spanish cooking here," some signs proudly proclaim), then Playa de las Américas is the place for you. New development continues apace, and persistent time-share touts are a constant nuisance at both resorts. The beaches are equipped with all water sports facilities but here too the emphasis is on sociable sunbathing. Many people simply opt for their hotel or apartment poolside or head for **Aguapark Octopus**, where a variety of waterslides

The dragon tree of Icon—a primitive survivor aged between 500 and 3,000 years old.

and chutes make getting soaked a creative venture. Nightlife is aimed at the 18- to 24-year-old market, and good-natured bois-terousness can sometimes spill over into rowdiness.

Other attractions in this area include **Cactus Park**, which claims the largest collection of its kind in the world, and **Go-kart racing**, both just off the motorway. There is also a small aquarium on the main promenade at Playa de las Américas.

West of Puerto

A full-day outing from Puerto de la Cruz along the unspoiled north and west coasts covers some of the island's most spectac-ular sights and scenery.

In the heart of banana plantations and vineyards sleepy Icod de Los Vinos is a place of pilgrimage for every coach tour party. They all come to gape at the **Drago Milenario** (1,000-year-old Dragon Tree), and no matter how many pictures you may have already seen of this botanical freak the real thing is still a wondrous sight. Wander round the small, picturesque squares behind the tree before leaving Icod.

Continue west on the coast road from Icod to **Garachico** and after 6 km (3½ miles) the tortuous descent begins. There are marvellous views looking directly down onto this com-pact little town, which is set on a small peninsula with the waves crashing all around.

The peninsula is actually formed from the volcanic debris that was deposited following a disastrous eruption in 1706, when most of the town and its inhabitants were destroyed. The best place to survey the aftermath of the petrified lava is from the beautifully preserved 16th-century **Castillo de San Miguel**. A lucky survivor, this fortress is now devoted to handicraft sales. Despite the destruction, Garachico is a little gem. Neat houses boasting typically attractive Canarian bal-conies line cobbled streets and old churches adorn pretty

Fuel types for cars/trucks: unleaded (*sin plomo*), **regular** (*gasolina*), **premium** (*super*), **diesel** (*gas-oil*)

squares. There is also a good choice of restaurants.

Farther along the coast road you reach Buenavista del Norte, and 8 km (5 miles) due west of here lies the most westerly point on Tenerife, the **Punta de Teno**. From here there are panoramic views across to Gomera and looking south to the massive cliffs of Los Gigantes (see below).

Turn back to Buenavista and take a marked turn up to the picturesque tiny village of **Masca**. Looking down, you will be rewarded with some of the most dramatic scenery on the island. The road clings precariously to the side of lush, green mountains cleft by deep, dark ravines. Up to a few years ago the village could only be reached by donkey. Aside from a few touristy restaurants there is little here, but the setting is stupendous.

Rejoin the main road at Santiago del Teide and a little farther south turn off towards **Puerto de Santiago**. This is a new resort cultivating an upmarket clientele for whom watersports and messing about in boats are the main attractions. Walk out to the edge of the marina jetty to get the best view of the enormous sheer cliffs known appropriately as **Los Gigantes**. You can best appreciate the scale of this giant rockface when a boat passes by and is dwarfed into utter insignificance.

GRAN CANARIA
Area: 1,533 square km (592 square miles)
Population: 650,000

In spite of its name, Gran Canaria is only the third biggest of the Canary Islands. However, it is second to none for its perfect beaches and its sophisticated nightlife, for its history and hub-bub, marvellous natural scenery, sightseeing, and shopping.

Almost circular in shape, Gran Canaria is the classic volcanic cone in profile. It is small enough to get to know quite well within a week or two, yet its mountainous character causes the climate to change radically with latitude and altitude. You can leave a wet and chilly Las Palmas in the morning and an hour later be enjoying a hot, sunny day in Maspalomas.

Gran Canaria has been called a continent in miniature. The coastline ranges from awe-inspiring cliffs to golden dunes. Inland you can choose between stark mountains and tranquil valleys. Travelling from the din of Las Palmas to the peace of a languorous provincial village is almost likely to bring on culture shock.

Apart from its tourist industry Gran Canaria earns its living from agriculture. Under intensive cultivation, the soil produces crops of bananas, tomatoes, and potatoes to satisfy the appetites of those living in less temperate zones.

Las Palmas

Bustling Las Palmas, population 377,500, the largest city in the Canaries, is a major commercial and historical centre, a cosmopolitan resort, and a vital seaport all rolled into one.

Up to a thousand ships arrive at the port a month to take on fuel, unload cargo (these days mostly oil and petroleum) or just give the crew a break. Gone, however, are the romantic days of the 1960s and 1970s when grand liners such as the *Queen Elizabeth* and *Queen Mary* were regular visitors here. Due to the changing nature of cargo and port handling, the colourful presence of sailors of many nations is also less apparent now than it used to be. The main fleet in Puerto de la Luz these days is Korean. The port is not really a sightseeing area and the downbeat residential area of La Isleta should be avoided.

The real hub of Las Palmas is the **Parque de Santa Catalina**. This square is effectively one gigantic outdoor café and buzzes day and night with almost every language in the world. Exotically dressed visitors from West Africa sip tea or ply their wares, tourists with peeling noses down excesses of bargain-priced gin and brandy, and the Spaniards avidly digest the local and national newspapers.

It is a short walk through the dusty streets to **Playa de las Canteras.** This superb golden beach stretches for 3 to 5 km (2 to 3 miles) and a natural reef just offshore means that the water couldn't be calmer. Las Canteras and the area behind it

The coastal roads on Gran Canaria are often spectacular. View from south of Agaete.

reflect the city's cosmopolitan nature, with a bewildering assortment of restaurants of every nationality, from Bulgarian to Korean, British to Venezuelan. Like the city in general, though, it has seen better days and is losing younger tourist trade to the smarter modern resorts in the south.

Just south of Parque de Santa Catalina is the major traffic thoroughfare of Avenida de Mesa y López. This broad, tree-lined, shady avenue plays host to several market stalls and is also a major shopping street featuring stores such as El Corte Inglés and many international retailers.

The most colourful shopping in town is to be found on Sunday mornings at the town's large and lively *rastro* (flea market)

ket) held near the port. There are bargains galore. In addition, its many African vendors add an exotic atmosphere to the market.

Cheap and frequent buses (Canarians call them *guaguas*, pronounced "quah-quahs") run along the seafront from Avenida Marítima down to Triana. It is not only fun to go native by hopping on one, it is also the most sensible option in this traffic-choked city.

Make your first stop **Doramas Parque**, a pleasantly landscaped park named after a Guanche island chieftain. The statue in front of the park recalls the dangerous ancient sport of ravine-leaping, practised by local inhabitants in the distant past. At the rear of the park is the splendid colonial-style Hotel Casino Santa Catalina.

Adjacent to the park is the **Pueblo Canario** (Canary Village). This is a romanticized version of a Canarian village where you can shop for handicrafts and watch displays of folk dancing and singing. The Pueblo is pretty, very relaxed, and, in spite of its obviously artificial nature, still well worth a visit. The man who conceived it was local artist and designer Néstor de la Torre (1888–1938). A museum of his exotic art is in the Pueblo.

The bus terminal is at **Triana**, one of the older *barrios* (suburbs). Today it is known for its upmarket shops, and the long, pleasant, pedestrianized street of Calle Mayor de Triana offers just about everything for both tourists and locals.

Adjoining Triana is **Vegueta**, the oldest part of the city, where Spanish forces first set up camp in 1478. History lurks behind every wall and this is a delightful place just to wander around.

Christopher Columbus knew these streets, and he prayed at the **Ermita de San Antonio Abad** before setting off on his first Voyage of Discovery to the New World. The present building dates from the 18th century. Close by on Calle Colón is the beautiful 15th-century **Casa de Colón**. This elegant house with

LAS PALMAS DE GRAN CANARIA

its charming courtyard was formerly the residence of the island's first governor, and Columbus is said to have stayed here on three occasions. Now an atmospheric museum, it recreates the Age of Discovery with exhibits of navigational instruments, charts, weapons, and everyday items of the period.

Around the corner stands the vast Gothic and neo-Classic bulk of the **Catedral de Santa Ana**. While it could never be described as pretty it is certainly impressive, and is best seen by night when floodlighting softens its harsh, grimy front. For a few pesetas you may be able to see the treasury, with exhibits of ancient religious art and jewellery. Opening times, however, are rather erratic.

Facing the cathedral are several green bronze statues of the aboriginal mastiff dogs after whom the Canary Islands are said to have been named (from the Latin *canes*).

On the corner of Calle Doctor Chil and Calle Doctor Verneau is the rather self-effacing **Museo Canario**. The islands' most important collection from Guanche times is stored within its 12 rooms. The highlight is the room of skulls and mummies, depicting the Guanches' fascination with death (see page 12). The rest of the museum will appeal only to archaeological enthusiasts, and captions throughout are in Spanish.

Southern Exposure

The southern resorts of San Agustín, Playa del Inglés, and Maspalomas (often all lumped together under the collective name of Maspalomas) are linked to Las Palmas and Gran Canaria international airport by the fast and featureless *autopista* (motorway).

For some holidaymakers it is rather disconcerting to learn that this three-in-one resort is the biggest holiday complex in all of Spain, let alone the Canaries. Each resort does have its own characteristics, however.

San Agustín, the first stop off the *autopista*, is a restrained area of low-rise apartments, catering for more mature and discerning holidaymakers. Above, the streets are neat and tidy; below, there is a quiet, black-sand beach backed by low cliffs.

> **Full tank, please!**
> — *Llénelo, por favor.* (lyaynayloa por fahbhor)

Playa del Inglés is more robust, as the very name (Beach of the English) might suggest. In winter, though, there are just as many German visitors here. This is a fun-and-sun resort of high-rise hotels, shopping malls, and fast-food restaurants. It was built several years ago, and the raw concrete edges are being smoothed away by the brilliantly coloured local flora. The modern Ecumenical Church, shaped like the Sydney Opera House, also brings some interest to the skyline. For the less God-fearing the nightlife can be hectic, and at the last count there were more than 50 discos here. The golden beach stretches for 10 featureless miles (16 km) so there is room enough for everyone and all watersports are practised.

Maspalomas is famous for its **dunes,** which are sufficiently large and unspoiled to constitute a mini-Sahara of great

Canaries

You don't have to be an expert, or a canary, to tell the difference between a male and a female canary. Only the male knows how to sing.

Canaries, the most famous wildlife found in the islands, take their name from the archipelago, and not vice versa. They are also found on Madeira and the Azores.

Serinus canaria was first imported to Europe in the 16th century. Originally they were colourless birds, but breeders in Europe were able to develop a yellow variety and other festive colours followed. Your chances of spotting wild canaries today are slim. Look instead in the cages attached to the outside of houses in smaller towns and villages.

beauty. They are a protected nature reserve but you are far more likely to see naturists than naturalists here. Playa de Maspalomas is the stretch of dunes close to the landmark lighthouse and is home to a small number of top-class hotels and luxury *urbanizaciones*. As you might expect, there is the usual plethora of family attractions nearby, including go-karting, Ocean Park and Aqua Sur water parks, and the Holiday World amusement complex.

Palmitos Parque, situated in a picturesque gorge some 13 km (8 miles) north of Maspalomas, provides an excellent day out for all the family. Performing parrots amuse with circus tricks, and caged birds of every imaginable hue are kept in beautiful gardens. The real stars, however, are the exotic free-flying residents, including brilliantly coloured parrots and toucans.

The area's other major attraction is **Sioux City**, near San Agustín. This is a recreation of the Wild West, with gun-fights, lynchings, saloon gals, lassooing tricks, and so on. The evening show with barbecue is great fun for children.

West of Maspalomas, smaller developments are the norm, but in recent years these have been built so thick and fast that there has

An eagle-shaped balcony watches over a street in the bustling city of Las Palmas.

been an outcry from conservationists. Many apartments stand empty, and with such little beach space available it is hard to imagine they will ever be occupied. The charming fishing port of **Arguineguín** has managed to retain its identity, though adjacent Patalavaca is very highly developed.

Puerto Rico is the most attractive beach resort on this coast. It too has been grossly overdeveloped with holiday accommodation on all the surrounding hillsides, so its lovely, sheltered, golden beach can become unbearably crowded. Out of season, though, it is recommended. Puerto Rico is famous for its watersports and there is also an attractive marina here.

Puerto de Mogán should be an object lesson to all Canarian resort developers in how to provide accommodation that is functional, very attractive, and totally in sympathy with its surroundings. The holiday accommodation here is an interpretation of local town houses which are ablaze with bougain-villaea, and arranged in pedestrian-only squares with narrow alleyways and arches leading to an attractive marina. This is lined with stylish cafés and restaurants, jazz and piano bars, and small boutiques. All that is lacking is a good beach, but to

Keep your eyes peeled at Palmitos Parque for free-flying birds such as this toucan.

compensate, regular boat trips do shuttle to and from Puerto Rico.

A submarine trip also runs from here, but it is very expensive and there is little to see. One of the best nautical trips is an excursion aboard the *Windjammer San Miguel*, a fine old transatlantic sailing ship built in 1919. It departs daily from Puerto Rico for a cruise along the coast, and the trip includes lunch and stops for swimming.

Northern Coast and Hinterland

The northern coastal zone of Gran Canaria is banana land. Row upon row of green terraced plantations slope gently down from the mountains to the edge of the sea.

The centre of this activity is **Arucas**, a workaday white town overshadowed by an immense neo-Gothic cathedral. This titanic 20th-century creation stands out like a sore thumb. The road west from Arucas follows a truly dizzying route through the mountains past several caves. Some provide shelter for goats, but others are inhabited by people and are complete with running water and electricity. The route passes through the tidy small town of **Moya**. It is well worth stopping to see its church, precariously perched on the very edge of a ravine. An act of faith indeed!

Just off the coast road is the **Cenobio de Valerón** (Convent of Valerón). This is badly signposted. Take the turn off just before Guía, away from the sea. This convent is actually a series of Guanche caves cut into a steep mountainside. According to island lore, the daughters of noble families spent their youth in these small cells serving the native gods. At the age of 15 they were allowed to marry or to remain in the sanctuary for life. More prosaically the caves were probably also used for grain storage. Around this area, too, you will spy many modern cave dwellers.

Pass through **Guía**, a small, pretty town with a fine church, and continue to Gáldar. Here there are more Guanche connections. This was once a royal capital and there are two sites of interest. Frustratingly, neither is currently accessible. The Cueva Pintada (Painted Cave), with geometric Guanche patterns, is the subject of long-term restoration, and the Tumulo de la Guanche (a Guanche burial ground) is in a sorry state and behind a padlocked fence a little way out of town. Gáldar itself is a busy small town and certainly merits a coffee stop.

Continue south towards Agaete and after a few miles you will see the signs for **Reptilandia**. Perched on the edge of the Montaña Almagro, this small zoo specializes in lizards, snakes, and crocodiles but also has monkeys and assorted insects. **Agaete** is the most attractive of the small northern towns. It lies in a green and fertile region and boasts a small, shady botanic garden (Huerto de las Flores).

Agaete's port, **Puerto de las Nieves,** is a haven of calm among the formidable rocky cliffs that make up this inhospitable stretch of coast. A small promenade has been built, so perhaps the village is getting ready for a greater influx of tourists. Currently, though, it is a fine choice for a fish lunch, and the best view is from the **El Dedo de Dios** (Finger of God) restaurant. This looks out over the tiny beach where the small fishing fleet rest, to the slender rock pile pointing skywards from which the restaurant takes its name. (If the light is not falling on the "finger" in a certain way you may have to look twice to distinguish it from its rocky background.) The Ermita de las Nieves contains a 16th-century Flemish triptych and several model sailing ships.

From here the coast road ascends very sharply amid sparse, windblown greenery, and the drop seawards can be frighteningly steep. An alternative route is to drive 7 km (4 miles) inland to the fine viewpoint at **Los Berrazales**.

Central Sights

The mountainous centre of the island makes for very tiring driving. You will rarely get out of the lower gears, but the wonderful panoramas are ample reward. Pine forests, almond groves, gnarled mountains, sheer cliffs, and cloudy mountain tops beckon.

Arguably the best and certainly the most popular vantage point is the **Cruz de Tejeda** (Cross of Tejeda), at 1,463 meters (4,800 feet). This is one of the few points inland where you are almost guaranteed to meet fellow tourists. A small cluster of cafés, fruit and souvenir stalls, and a man with his donkeys wait at the summit for the coach parties. It is hardly high-pressure tourism, however, and the elegant *parador* (state-run restaurant) here is a welcome refreshment stop.

The magnificent panorama includes two rock formations that were once worshipped by the Guanches. The most distinctive is the statuesque **Roque Nublo** at 1,817 meters (5,961 feet); the other is the Roque Bentaiga.

As the Cruz de Tejeda is the hub of the island there are any number of routes to and from it and almost all have something to offer.

The road south to **Tejeda** itself looks right down onto the rooftops of this attractive village. It is the highest settlement on the island and is particularly attractive in February, when a delicate pink carpet of almond blossom covers the area. By contrast the dark, broody bulk of Roque Nublo draws ever closer, and it takes little imagination to understand the primitive inhabitants' fascination with this formation.

The village of Artenara to the northwest offers what is surely the best restaurant view on the island. The place in question is **Méson de la Silla**, not easy to spot, parallel to the main road. A dark tunnel leads through the rock with no hint of what is to come, then emerges on the other side of the mountain to a bright 180-degree mountain panorama. You can visit just to admire the view.

The road west leads to the **pine forest of Tamadaba**. On a clear day the view across to Mount Teide, floating majestically above the clouds, is magical. On a misty day, however, you may see nothing but pine trees.

If you are in a four-wheel-drive vehicle and don't mind negotiating hair-raising bends, take the road between Artenara and Tamadaba to Acusa. Way down below this spectacular track are several deep dark reservoirs. The road continues to the east coast via the market town of San Nicolás de Tolentino. There are more breathtakingly sited reservoirs to the south but these really are quite remote and are best visited on an organized four-wheel-drive vehicle excursion.

Northeast of the Cruz de Tejeda is the peaceful valley town of **Teror**. The old whitewashed houses, often built around graceful patios, boast fine traditional carved balconies. The major landmark here is a typically large Canarian church, the **Basilica Nuestra Señora del Pino** (Our Lady of the Pine). This commemorates the miraculous discovery in 1481 — in the branches of a pine tree — of a sacred effigy. The Blessed Virgin of Teror is also the patron saint of Gran Canaria.

Don't miss the main town museum, the **Casa de los Patronos de la Virgen del Pino**. Despite its religious name this attractive 18th-century house displays everyday artefacts from the past and is deceptively spacious.

For panoramic views of the east of the island head northeast from the Cruz de Tejeda through the towns of Vega de San Mateo and Santa Brígida. Because the micro-climate here is exceptionally mild, many Canarians and foreign residents have built very desirable homes in these hills. The gardens around their villas are often magnificent.

The **Caldera de Bandama** nearby is one of the island's finest natural features. This volcanic crater, almost a kilometer (more than a half mile) across, is green and fertile. Farm buildings nestle at the bottom, some 198 meters (650 feet) down, in a scene reminiscent of a sleepy Alpine valley. A scenic spiralling road leads to the top, where the Real Club de Golf enjoys such a picturesque location that even non-golfers are tempted to pick up a club.

On Gran Canaria you can even see wonderful scenery just off the *autopista*. Exit at Carrizal, about half way between Las Palmas and Maspalomas, make the short journey to Agüimes and the handicraft-town of Ingenio, and you will discover the locally celebrated **Barranco de Guyadeque**. This spectacular ravine is famous for its caves and is best explored on a group excursion. The road inland from Ingenio offers fine views.

A few miles north is Gran Canaria's second city, **Telde**. This was the capital of Doramas, king of the Guanche chieftains. Today it is badly congested with traffic, but is still an attractive colonial city of genteel houses famous for their balconies. The late-15th-century Iglesia de San Juan de Bautista is thought to be the oldest church on the island.

LANZAROTE
Area: 803 square km (310 square miles)
Population: 75,000

Lanzarote is a startling island, representing the triumph of civilization over a hostile environment. Its pock-marked, lunar-like surface is dotted with more than 300 volcanoes, yet onions, potatoes, tomatoes, melons, and grapes all spring in abundance from the black ash. The daily scene of Lanzaroteños (or Conejeros as they are sometimes called) toiling successfully in such an apparently desolate landscape warms the heart. It is not only in the fields that the island is succeeding. Newer to the tourist scene than either Gran Canaria or Tenerife, Lanzarote seems to have learned from the excesses of its sister islands. Here, small is beautiful and harmony with the environment is the philosophy.

The South of the Island

Arrecife, the point of arrival for most visitors, unfortunately sets a very poor example for the island and it is probably as well that most people head straight out of it. This principal port and latter-day capital is a characterless place with just two saving graces — the Castillo de San Gabriel and the Castillo de San José.

The 16th-century **Castillo de San Gabriel**, situated on an islet close to the centre of town, houses a small museum of no great standing. But it is worth the walk, across the small drawbridge and over the lagoon, onto the small island from where the castle used to deter pirates.

Follow the coast road for several kilometers (a couple of miles) and, just past the fishing port, you'll come to the **Castillo de San José**, a far more interesting proposition.

Burglary at the Basilica

On 17 January 1975, the richly robed, bejewelled, and crowned statue of Madonna and Child was the target of one of the most sensational (and professional) crimes in Canaries' history. Burglars broke through the 200-year-old ceiling of the church and stripped the most important diamonds, sapphires, and gold and silver votive adornments from the statue. They left behind many items considered less valuable — or impossible to dispose of. Estimates on the haul range from 10–20 million pesetas.

For a small charge you can enter the treasury of the church and see the statue of the patron saint on her silver throne. Buy a pre-robbery postcard and you will have some idea of just how much jewellery was taken.

Built in the 18th century, this well-preserved fortress now houses the late César Manrique's small but impressive International Museum of Contemporary Art, which includes works by Picasso and Miró. There is also a fine restaurant with panoramic sea views.

The island's major resort is **Puerto del Carmen**. Its long golden beach stretches for about 5 km (3 miles) and comfortably accommodates its visitors. The sea is calm and ideal for families. Restaurants, bars, and shops line the Avenida de las Playas, Lanzarote's one outbreak of mass commercialism. Yet Spanish bars and restaurants can still be found on "the strip," and though there is a healthy nightlife scene the people in the apartments a block or so back from the beach may well be oblivious to it.

The **old town** just west of the beach has a charming small harbour area with traditional bars and restaurants. On the hill above it the **Montaña Tropical**, a modern complex of shops, bars, and restaurants, provides good family entertainment day and night. Flamenco dancers, performing parrots, and folklore and handicraft displays all find a stage here.

The road west leads through the beautifully tended village of Yaiza to the rather more earthy **Salinas de Janubio** (salt flats at Janubio). On a bright day the dazzling white of the drying salt set against the azure blue of the sea and the black volcanic soil can produce an impressive natural work of art. There is even a *mirador* restaurant overlooking the flats.

A little farther north are two more natural spectacles. Los Hervideros is a section of rocky coast where the crashing waves break ferociously against the cliffs and sea caves. You must visit on a very blustery day to appreciate it fully.

El Golfo, by contrast, is a placid, emerald-green lagoon set beneath a cliffside which resembles a gigantic petrified tidal wave just about to break. This is actually the inner rim of a volcanic cone, half of which has disappeared beneath the sea. The strata, colours, and manic whirls are a fascinating sight. Note that El Golfo is not apparent from the roadside. Park your car on the rough ledge, just off the main road on the left as you begin the descent into the village of El Golfo (renowned for the quality of its fish restaurants), and follow the rough footpath over the cliff.

The newly created resort of **Playa Blanca** on the south coast is host to a marina as well as the Fuerteventura ferry and hydrofoil. There is a good golden beach here, but as yet building work is far from complete in the resort. However, just a few miles east along unmade roads are the best sands on the island, collectively known as the **Papagayo (parrot) beaches**. You will need a four-wheel-drive vehicle, local directions (there are no signposts), and little else, as on Papagayo naturism is the norm. There is a large, popular beach and several secluded coves.

The Magic of Manrique

César Manrique was Lanzarote's greatest artist, designer, landscaper, conservationist, and all-round cultural mandarin. Trained primarily in Madrid, he was born here in 1920 and died in 1992 in a car crash; there is hardly a visitor attraction that does not bear his signature in some way.

In his own words, his works were "dreams that capture the sublime natural beauty of Lanzarote," and he constantly strived to ensure that tourist developments were in harmony with the island's character. Simplicity was the key — whitewashed walls, natural building materials, classical or local music, and local food and wine are the Manrique hallmarks.

His own home Taro Tahiche at Tahiche, 7 km (4 miles) due north of Arrecife, is now open to the public.

The highlight of your trip to Lanzarote and the magical ingredient that makes this island so special is to be found in the **Montañas del Fuego** (Mountains of Fire). The Parque Nacional de Timanfaya, which encompasses the mountains, starts just north of Yaiza, and its boundary is marked by an impish devil motif. This desolate national park was formed largely over the course of 16 cataclysmic months during 1730 and 1731. Eleven villages were buried forever and many of the people left the island for Gran Canaria.

Just inside the *malpaís* (volcanic badlands) of the park, **camels** take tourists on a short ride up and down a volcanic hill. Whether or not you think the ride is worthwhile, the hubbub in the car park (which doubles as a "camel park") when busy is not to be missed. Chaotic, colourful, and quite exotic, it could almost be a North African bazaar. Camels were once used as beasts of burden in the fields of Lanzarote, but you will be very fortunate to see one at work these days.

Drive on and turn left at the small roundabout to the Montañas del Fuego where you buy an admission ticket. Your introduction to the inner sanctum of the mountains leaves no doubt that at least one of these volcanoes (in fact the very one that you are standing on!) is not dead, just sleeping. A guide demonstrates this by pouring water down a tube into the earth, then beating a hasty retreat. Seconds later a geyser erupts, startling the diners in the adjacent restaurant. You can watch the food being cooked over an enormous barbecue that uses the volcano as its fuel — a source that is timeless, limitless, and, of course, free.

Cars are not allowed any farther into the park, and from here coach tours (included in the admission price) depart to explore the incredible landscape. Any badlands that you may have seen up to this point have been a mere appetiser for the main course. The words *lunar* and *alien* are worked to exhaustion in attempts to describe the area and still scarcely do justice to the dramatic scenery. Suffice it to say that when the theme music to the film *2001* is played on the coach at the end of your tour, you will be convinced that you have just visited another world.

With rain so rare and underground water sources extremely limited you may wonder how Lanzarote manages to survive as an agricultural island. The black topsoil is the secret, discovered by the farmers in their adversity. The porous volcanic particles that make up the topsoil are useless in themselves but act as a sponge for the moisture of the night air, obtaining water for the plants and eliminating the need for rain. They are therefore piled on top of the crops and only need replacing around once every 20 years. The other Canary Islands also use this method.

The most impressive example of this type of farming is the vineyards around the valley of **La Geria**. Each vine is set in its own mini-crater, protected from wind and excess sun by a low semi-circular wall of lava stones (other crops are also protected in this manner). The horseshoe patterns thus formed stretch way up the mountains and apparently into infinity, producing an almost hypnotic effect. Not only do the vineyards look good, the end product also tastes very good, and there are several *bodegas* in the Geria valley where you can sample the excellent local *malvasía*.

The North of the Island

The geographic centre of Lanzarote lies 9 km (5½ miles) northwest of the capital at Mozaga, focal point of the island's viniculture. Here the late César Manrique designed and erected a huge white modern sculpture, **Monumento al Campesino**, dedicated to the peasant workers of the island. Adjacent to this towering landmark is a small rural museum. You can sample the fruits of the fields either from the shop or in the restaurant.

The road continues via Tiagua and Tinajo to La Santa. On your island travels you may well have seen muscle-bound cyclists on the roads, and as you near La Santa you will probably see some extremely professional-looking joggers and sprinters. Club La Santa is a time-share development resort where athletes of the highest level come for both training and relaxation; almost every sport is covered at this resort of the super-fit.

A few miles north of La Santa is the pleasant beach of Famara, backed by the high cliffs of the Famara Massif. The currents can be dangerous here, so take care.

Teguise is a fine old town of cobbled streets and gracious mansions and was the island capital until 1852. Now it is calm and quiet for six days of the week. On Sundays a **handicrafts market** comes to town where you can buy a *timple*

Desolate trek — two hikers traverse the sand dunes of Maspalomas on Gran Canaria.

— a small ukulele-like instrument used by local folklore musicians. Several of its old buildings have been converted to craft and antique shops and restaurants.

Overlooking the town is the 16th-century **Castillo de Santa Bárbara**. The views from this wind-blown point are worth the trip alone. High on top of the extinct volcano of Guanapay, the castle now hosts the Museo del Emigrante Canario. Here sepia photos and nostalgic exhibits tell the sad story of how mass emigration to South America was the only option left for many Canarian families.

Costa Teguise, just north of Arrecife, is a totally modern resort, comprising several *urbanizaciónes* with time-shares, hotels, and apartments designed for a wealthy client-tele. There is a handful of good sandy beaches, particularly Playa de las Cucharas, where watersports thrive and windsurfing is particularly popular. A championship golf course, the Acua Lanza water park, and various other sporting facilities mean that no one need ever be bored here.

The coast road east passes the town of Guatiza, where prickly pears abound and where cochineal beetles are still cultivated (see page 17). César Manrique also cultivated the spiny flora into a beautiful **Jardín de Cactus**, complete with a working windmill which produces its own *gofio* (see page 13).

There is more Manrique design to admire at the caves of **Jameos del Agua**, where his landscaping tal-

A Lanzaroteña dressed in typical bonnet and headscarf as protection against wind and dust.

ents have embellished and transformed a grotto and underground lagoon into a short fantasy journey. Ethereal mood
music accompanies your descent into the cave, lushly planted with luxuriant foliage. Peer into the black lagoon and
you can pick out the extremely rare tiny albino spider crabs
that live here. Finally you emerge from the cave into a South
Seas paradise. In the evening the Jameos del Agua is transformed into a night club where folklore shows are regularly
staged.

The adjacent **Cueva de los Verdes** (Green Cave) is part of
the same system, blasted through the earth by exploding
lava. There is a guided tour that includes some memorable
sound and light effects that evoke the menacing volcano
most effectively.

At the northern tip of the island is the small fishing port of
Orzola. This is the embarkation point for the tiny island of
Graciosa. With superb beaches and a complete lack of tourist
development this is the place to get away from it all for the
day.

For an unforgettable view of **Isla Graciosa**, and much more,
drive up to the **Mirador del Río**. You have to pay to gain admission to this lookout point, but it is probably the most spectacular
mirador in all the Canaries — and yet another Manrique creation. Way down below, the incongruous bright pink square in
the otherwise blue and beige panorama is a salt pan.

Another addition to the island's burgeoning tourist attractions is the **Guinate Tropical Bird Park** just south of the
Mirador del Río. Over 300 different feathered species are on
display in lovely landscaped gardens, while performing parrots entertain in the theatre.

Overall the north of the island is substantially greener
than the badlands of the south, and nowhere is this more apparent than around **Haría**. With its tiny, white, pristine hous-

es scattered around "The Valley of 1,000 Palms," the scenery is reminiscent of a North African oasis town. The road south boasts more *miradors* to enhance your enjoyment of this delightful area.

FUERTEVENTURA
Area: 2,020 square km (780 square miles)
Population: 28,000

Beaches on Fuerteventura still outnumber hotels. At the last count there were 152 pristine golden stretches surrounding this arid rock. The island is situated less than 96 km (60 miles) off the coast of North Africa, and most of its sand is blown here from the Sahara, giving a new meaning to the term "desert island."

Fuerteventura is barren and windswept almost to the point of desolation — or grandeur, depending on your point of view. Its landscape may not have the variety and contrasts of

A local lugs his basket up a hillside on Lanzarote — work that might have been done by camels in an earlier era.

neighbouring Lanzarote but most travellers still find some inspiration in its primeval appearance.

In ancient times Fuerteventura was called Herbania, on account of its lush vegetation. Today's visitors may find this simply too farfetched to believe. But that was before the "civilizing" European invaders depleted the pasturelands with their livestock and cut down the forests for ship timbers. Ecological disaster followed in the form of erosion and drought. Many centuries later, growth is recommencing, but still in many places even the cacti look as if they need to be watered. Goats survive better here than people and, at some 60,000 strong, outnumber the human inhabitants by two to one.

The wind whistles with great force in Fuerteventura and may even have given the island its name, a corruption and inversion of *el viento fuerte* (the strong wind). However, it is a wind that seems to be bringing good fortune to the island, as the presence of so many windsurfers proves. With the growth of tourism the island has become one of the world's leading windsurfing centres.

The North

The once sleepy fishing port of **Corralejo** has been transformed into the busy Lanzarote ferry terminal and a bustling resort popular with the British. There is one main street, an uninspired *Centro Comercial* and a pleasant, pedestrianized square. Here, cafés and restaurants surround a bandstand, and musical and folklore performers provide a lively atmosphere. The old port area still has colourful fishing boats and some good fish restaurants.

Corralejo is famous for its magnificent long white beach and **dunes,** which lie a five-minute drive from the port through a fairly dense concentration of apartment development. The dunes, stretching for some 30 square km (12 square miles), have been declared a National Park and are popular with nudists.

The **Isla de los Lobos** lies 3 km (2 miles) offshore, and its beaches are even more secluded than those on the "mainland." The fishing here is outstanding. Glass-bottomed ferry boats depart regularly from Corralejo.

Another place to go to get away from it all (though you may not feel the need to on Fuerteventura) is **El Cotillo**. This tiny fishing village on the east coast also boasts some excellent beaches, plus a handful of local bars and some basic restaurants. Just west of El Cotillo is the lace-making town of Lajares.

The small town of **La Oliva** south of Corralejo is not especially attractive but it does feature two places of interest. Just off the main road stands the Casa de los Coroneles (House of the Colonels). Its name derives from its 18th-century tenants who once ruled the island. The decaying, cream-coloured building still exudes a certain haughty, if melancholy, grandeur. By contrast, the nearby Centro de Arte Canario is bright and modern, exhibiting the works of some of the finest living Canarian artists.

Puerto del Rosario, the island's capital, has nothing of interest for tourists. However, just south of here is the new cosmopolitan development of **El Castillo** (also known as **Caleta de Fuste**). Activities focus around the marina and the attractive, horseshoe-shaped beach, where windsurfing is a particularly popular sport.

The Central Area

As you drive south you will see that occasional oases do exist amid the arid mountain ranges. There are clumps of palm trees, potato patches, and tomato groves. The latter can be quite large and are often covered so that they resemble huge greenhouses. From the high roads (particularly between Betancuria and Pájara) these appear as large, incongruously regular, silvery oblongs on the landscape. Long, thin tomato canes, stacked to dry in wooden wigwams, are also a common sight.

Betancuria, the most attractive and most visited inland town on the island, is one of the aforementioned oases. Although the river bed here is almost perpetually dry, the town

> *Betancuria, named after the island conqueror Jean de Béthencourt, was the capital of the island in medieval times; today it is a charming village disturbed only by curious tourists.*

is fortunate in having a high water table. Because of its theoretical invulnerability at the heart of the island it was made Fuerteventura's first capital in the early 15th century. However, in 1539 somehow the ravaging Berber pirates overcame the mountains (which still provide a difficult drive even today) and destroyed the original cathedral. The present 17th-century church, **Iglesia de Santa María**, is a splendid building and hosts many interesting treasures. As the keeper of the church also looks after the Museo de Arte Sacro across the square, you may need to buy a combined ticket to see inside. Adjacent to the museum is a leather factory-cum-shoe-shop, set in an atmospheric old building. Wander round this lovely little town and admire the view from across the bridge, where there is an unpretentious restaurant/bar and a gift shop.

Just south of Betancuria is the neat and pretty village of **Pájara**. Its charming tiny church features a beautiful stone portal carved with flowing Aztec patterns and imagery. Look into the church, then go next door and have a coffee with the locals in the Centro Cultural.

The South

Tarajalejo is nominally a resort, but of little interest, and the town of Gran Tarajal in fact sounds far grander than it has a right to — which leaves the 26-km- (16-mile-) long sandy shores of **Jandía** to be explored.

At the northern tip of the Jandía sands are the beautiful beaches of **Costa Calma**, not blighted as yet by overdevelopment. Here, a low cliff backing and a scattering of rocks and coves give the beach far more character than some of the seemingly endless stretches farther south.

The **Playa de Sotavento** is world-famous as a windsurfing centre, with activity focused on the F2 school at the Los Goriones Hotel. Here the beach is very wide and flat, usually empty

Costa Calma, southern Fuerteventura,
where the beaches are long, golden, and as yet
unblighted by urbanization.

and, as the tides go out, also very wet. The **dunes** behind and a
little farther to the south form an idyllic beach backdrop.

Urbanizaciones spread relentlessly all the way down the
coast to **Morro del Jable**. This small town dips down to the
sea along a dry riverbed and a small promenade offers a
good choice of bars and restaurants. There are more fine
beaches towards the southern tip of the island but you will
need a four-wheel-drive vehicle to get there.

GOMERA

Area: 372 square km (146 square miles)
Population: 17,000

The short journey across the water from the crowded, throb-
bing resorts of south Tenerife to the island of Gomera can

take as little as 40 minutes. But in tourism terms it is a step back in time of many decades.

Of all the "Fortunate Islands" Gomera may be the luckiest, since it is the only one without a commercial airport. While tourism has picked up dramatically in recent years, Gomera nevertheless remains unspoiled and authentic, with its steep, green, terraced hills and tranquil valleys. In this world of irreversible "progress" you may be relieved to find roads completely free of advertising signs, *urbanizaciones,* and souvenir stalls.

For most tourists, a visit to Gomera means a boat and coach excursion from Tenerife. A vehicle/passenger ferry departs from Los Cristianos at around 10:00 A.M., and 75 minutes later disgorges its tourists at San Sebastián. From here it is on to a waiting coach and a whistle-stop tour that covers about half the island. The ferry returns to Tenerife at around 6:00 P.M. This is certainly a good introduction to Gomera and cuts out a day of exhausting driving. Independent travellers should catch the quicker hydrofoil, which takes only 40 minutes and makes more frequent crossings. To see the island properly you need at least two days.

San Sebastián

Capital and main port of the island, this small town (population 6,000) will always be important as the place where Columbus took leave of the known world on 6 September 1492, on the voyage which revealed the New World.

The Columbiana starts in the main square. A pavement mosaic shows the route of Colombus's voyage, and next to the large tree is the Casa de Aduana (the old Customs House). According to folklore, Columbus drew water from the well here, took it to the New World, and used it to baptize America.

Leading off the square, the **Calle del Medio** is the only street of any consequence in town and features more connections with the great navigator. The **Iglesia de la Asunción**, built between 1490–1510, looks and feels so old that you can easily imagine Columbus praying in a dark recess — which is what a plaque here tells us he did, in 1492. A little way up the street is the modest Casa Columbina/Casa de Colón, which is supposedly where he stayed in Gomera. Exhibitions are held here.

All historical connections aside, there are some interesting old-fashioned shops on the Calle del Medio and some surprisingly good restaurants. Another meal-time option is the excellent *parador,* which sits high above the town.

The North

The road from San Sebastián climbs steeply and the views soon become quite dizzying. The highest peak on Gomera, Alto de

---

The Lady in the Tower

Why did Columbus choose Gomera to set sail from? Some say because it was the most westerly staging point known at that time, others point to a certain Beatriz de Bobadilla. Columbus certainly knew this Spanish beauty, and history indicates that she was quite free with her favours. You can ponder on this while contemplating the Torre del Conde (Tower of the Count) a little way further on from the main square.

The Count in question, Hernán Peraza, the husband of Beatriz, was murdered one night at a mountain pass subsequently known at the Degollada de Peraza (the slaughter of Peraza). It seems that he had been leaving a native love nest and angry Guanches had ambushed him. Fearing an uprising by the local people, Beatriz retreated to the Tower and may well have entertained Columbus here. The building has not changed much in 500 years, although its present stranded site does leave much to be desired.

Garajonay is 1,487 meters (4,878 feet) — this is no great height by Canaries standards, yet the island often gives the impression of being a fearsome maze of eerie crags. One hilltop may be within waving distance of the next but driving between them on the main roads is a dizzying ordeal of twists and turns.

The small town of Hermigua is the largest on the island after San Sebastián. Stop at the crafts centre of **Los Telares** and take a look down into its green and fertile valley. Trellised vines crisscross the hillside in a cobweb-like maze and bananas and dates are cultivated. Ask if you can try the local liqueur, *mistela*, and watch women making blankets and rugs on their antique looms.

Agulo is a pleasant small town whose main feature is the domed Iglesia San Marco, which adjoins a monumental laurel tree in the plaza. This church was originally a mosque during a brief period of Moorish occupation in the 17th century.

A turn inland just before the village of Las Rosas is one of the entrances to the **Garajonay National Park**. There is an informa-

Whistle Down The Wind

The problem of being so close and yet so far, and how to communicate across the hilltops, was solved a long time before the telephone came to Gomera. For ages, gossip and messages have been transmitted across the ravines by the language of *el silbo* (the whistle). This is a real language of regulated tones and rhythms, representing words, whistled with or without the aid of fingers in the mouth, at great volume. Only a small minority of Gomerans keep the language alive. Many younger people may understand it, but they cannot converse in *silbo*. If you do not go on a coach tour that takes you to see *silbo* in action, try Las Rosas restaurant at the village of the same name, or the parador at San Sebastián, where the gardeners may be able to oblige you.

tion centre with a small museum and displays, and craft demonstrations are given to coach parties. The road continues to the Laguna restaurant, a hospitable, rough-and-ready sort of place, which is very popular with walkers. Unlike the National Parks at the peaks of many of the Canary islands, there are no views from here (aside from at Garajonay itself), and during the winter a thick mist clings to the ancient, moss-covered trees.

A curiosity just off the north coast is **Los Organos**, accessible only by boat. It consists of thousands of regularly shaped basalt columns rising from the sea like the pipes of some mighty organ. Trips leave from the south of the island and you may be able to hire a fishing boat from the beach nearest to Hermigua.

Windmills are a standard sight on the windswept Canaries.

The South

The main road from San Sebastián leads past three mighty volcanic plugs, which are nicknamed "the Chinese Hat," "the Lion," and "the Face of Christ" after their respective outlines. The windy pass of **Degollada de Peraza** offers spectacular views to both the north and the south. Continue to **Garajonay**, the highest point on the island, where you can enjoy more stunning views, or turn left to Playa de Santiago, the island's only beach resort.

Continue on the main road and away to the left looms the huge rock outcrop known as La Fortaleza, thought to have been held sacred by the indigenous Guanches. The village of El Cercado and its neighbouring hamlets are renowned for their pottery, which is produced completely by hand.

The highlight of the south is the beautiful, multi-tiered valley of **Valle Gran Rey**. Here on steep, steep terraces, avocados, pineapples, and dates are grown, in addition to the usual crops. Palm honey, produced from the milky palm sap, is a local speciality, but also available in other places on the island.

LA PALMA
Area: 725 square km (280 square miles)
Population: 80,000

La Palma, the most northwesterly of the Canaries, has two nicknames — La Isla Bonita and La Isla Verde. Beautiful it certainly is, and very green too. Development is strictly controlled, and unnecessary light is even kept from the night sky so that the famous La Palma observatory may function unhindered by artificial light sources.

Not only is the island beautiful but its statistics are very impressive too. The highest peak, Roque de los Muchachos, rises 2,423 meters (7,950 feet) above sea level, making it the steepest island in the world in relation to its total area.

At the heart of La Palma is the Caldera de Taburiente, a giant crater 9 km (5½ miles) wide and 701 meters (2,300 feet) deep. It was created some 400,000 years ago and has since been colonized by nature into a green, fertile valley.

☞ Santa Cruz de la Palma

The island capital (population 18,000) is an appealing metropolis in miniature — clean and bright with traditional and modern architecture side by side.

The heart of the town is the small triangular **Plaza de España**, set a couple of streets in from the seafront on the Calle Real. On one side of the triangle is the Iglesia Matriz de El Salvador (Church of the Saviour), built in 1503. The ceiling of this big stone church is made of *tea* (heart of pine) and is a fine example of the Mudejar (Muslim under Christian rule) style of intricate wooden panelling.

Next to the church are some splendid examples of 18th-century colonial-style mansions. The longest side of the triangle is taken up by the **ayuntamiento** (Town Hall), built in 1569. While the arches are Italian Renaissance, the interior (which you are free to inspect) is Spanish colonial, with formidable carved wooden ceilings and doors and a ceremonial staircase.

The **Calle Real** is a delightful street in which to stroll and enjoy the atmosphere. At its southern end it takes on the improbable title of Calle O'Daly, named after an Irish banana merchant who settled on the island. Even more improbably, right at the other end of the street looms a life-size model of Columbus's ship, the *Santa Maria*. This concrete and timber replica houses a small **naval museum** with

LA PALMA

maritime memorabilia dating from the 17th and 18th centuries.

Due to the steep, dorsal-shaped nature of the island there are only two main island routes to follow: the loop south of the Caldera de Taburiente or the loop north of it. The southern route is the more interesting of the two.

The Southern Loop

Las Nieves is a village built on the mountainside. The first indication of it is a roadside bar, followed by the 17th-century **Santuario de Nuestra Señora de las Nieves** (Sanctuary of Our Lady of the Snows). This holds the venerated 14th-century terracotta image of the Virgen de las Nieves, which relates to an ancient miracle when the Virgin appeared in Rome during snow in August. Every five years the image is carried to Santa Cruz in a procession known as *La Bajada de la Virgen* (the Descent of the Virgin).

A well-surfaced road leads through steep hills, offering superb vistas over the island and down to the sea. Just before you turn off the main road right towards La Cumbrecita there is a sign to the Ermita de la Virgen del Pino. This is well worth a small diversion, not so much for the building but for its *mirador* situation.

Shortly after joining the road to La Cumbrecita look to your right and you will notice the clouds cascading down the sides of the mountains like a waterfall. A local restaurant (a little farther on the main road) is named the Cascada after this effect.

Finally the road climbs into a craggy forest surrounded by mist-shrouded peaks with tall pines clinging to the most precarious ledges. This is **Caldera de Taburiente** country, where you are inside an extinct volcano. There are wonderful views from here, including the Roque de los Muchachos and the monolithic Roque Idafe, said to have been the sacred altar of the first Guanche natives on the island.

You can enjoy the Caldera by car but to get the most from the area you have to walk. One of the easiest routes into the Caldera starts further west at the Barranco de Las Angustias (Gorge of Anguish) and goes all the way to the Roque Idafe.

The main road passes west through the city of Los Llanos de Aridane. This modern agricultural centre is more notable for its surrounding countryside than anything else. In January and February the almond blossom brings a riot of pink to the hillsides.

Puerto de Tazacorte on the west coast features that rarest of La Palma commodities, a good beach. This small, black, sandy strip will never attract coachloads of sunbathers but it is a pleasant enough place, with a couple of bars and restaurants. Just north of here is the **Mirador del Time**. A few miles south lies another beach resort, Puerto Naos, which provides fine swimming.

The road south passes through San Nicolás. La Palma's volcanic eruption of 1949 sent an ever-widening stream of molten lava rushing down the green hillside here. You can see it now, petrified and black; the road runs right through the once deadly mass.

Just south of Fuencaliente there are even more recent signs of volcanic activity. The volcano of **Teneguía** erupted here in 1971, fortunately without casualties. Feel the ground — it is still warm! Don't confuse this with the adjacent larger cone of the Volcán de San Antonio, which exploded some three centuries earlier. You'll start to appreciate the volcanic soil if you sample the local wine, cultivated in the ash here.

Heading back north towards Santa Cruz is the Cueva de Belmaco. This is said to have been a meeting place of the an-

EL HIERRO

Punta del Guanche

Ensenada el Golfo

Tamaduste

Valverde

La Peña

Aeropuerto

Punta de la Dehesa

Los Llanillos Frontera

Puerto de la Estaca

Sabinosa

Mirador de Jinama

1500 Malpaso

Cabo Bonanza

aro de Orchilla

Taibique

N

5   10 km

5 miles

La Restinga

Punta Restinga

cient Guanche tribes, and large stones feature strange inscriptions, which archaeologists have been unable to interpret.

The final place of interest on this route is **Mazo**, famous locally for its pottery. Find the Cerámico Molino to see pottery made in the old Guanche way.

The Northern Loop

This serpentine road runs through the agricultural centre of Los Sauces to the north coast and the fishing villages around **Barlovento**. The goal for most travellers north is the **Roque de los Muchachos**. Follow the signs to the Observatoria de Astrofisica. You cannot go in the observatory but even a glimpse of this space-age building is memorable.

EL HIERRO

Area: 287 square km (107 square miles)
Population: 7,500

A daily 35-minute flight connects the island with Tenerife but tourist traffic is very limited. There are hardly any tourist facilities, no natural spectacles, and no good beaches. On the plus side, El Hierro is pretty, quiet, and totally unspoiled. For many travellers the latter is reason enough to visit this tiny rock.

The configuration of the roads makes exploration a frustrating affair. It is impossible to make a circular tour as roads just do not join up; for example, the beach of Las Casitas and the Mirador de la Peña are only half a kilometer (a third of a mile) apart as the crow flies, but you have to make a tortuous journey of some 30 km (18 miles) to get from one to the other.

Valverde

A ten-minute drive from the airport leads to the only Canaries capital located inland. The town of Valverde was built high on a mountainside to protect it from pirate raids. Despite a population of some 3,600 inhabitants, Valverde is a very small town, with only a parador and four other places offering tourist accommodation. Nevertheless, there is a tourist office and, next door to that, a small museum.

The Rest of the Island

From Valverde follow the road to Isora, a neat little village of well-tended gardens. You are more likely to hear the tinkle of goat bells here than the rumble of another internal combustion engine

There are three *miradors* to enjoy on the road to El Pinar. The name comes from the pinewood forests which in places make up a gentle rolling landscape of fields and trees reminiscent of northern Europe.

As the road descends south the greenery eventually peters out into volcanic badlands. At the tip of the island is the fishing port of La Restinga, with a large, unattractive harbour wall.

The switchback road down to Frontera passes fertile cultivated fields and the occasional disused *lagar* (wine press). The belltower of the church here is something of an oddity, being divorced from its body and set on top of a small hill next to it. From a distance the tiny tower set against the massive cliffside seems terribly remote, but as you approach it the illusion disappears and the main road passes within feet of the church and tower. The cliffs here, and all along the stretch of north coast known as **El Golfo**, are actually part of an immense volcanic crater, half of which is beneath the sea.

The road west leads to the village of Sabinosa where the Casa de Huespedes serves good basic local food. Just south of here, though only accessible by a long journey, is the Ermita de los Reyes and the forest of **El Sabinal**. The forest is made up of juniper trees (*sabinosas*) which are incredibly and grotesquely twisted, stunted, gnarled, and, in some cases, almost bent double by the wind.

The **Mirador de la Peña**, 8 km (5 miles) west of Valverde, is the newest, the most impressive, and arguably the only real tourist attraction on the island. Those familiar with the work of César Manrique (see page 50) will need no introduction. The views are marvellous and the restaurant stands head and shoulders above anything else on the island, both in terms of altitude and cuisine (with the possible exception of the remote *parador* south of Valverde).

If you want to escape the crowds, try El Hierro, where good beaches are scarce, but so are other tourists.

WHAT TO DO

SPORTS

With the wonderfully mild climate of the Canaries, most sports are a year-round pleasure. Although water sports obviously dominate the scene there are some surprises — from Canaries wrestling to parachuting. If you are a dedicated sports enthusiast consider staying at the Club La Santa on Lanzarote, where just about every sport on and off the water is catered for.

Fishing: From the number of islanders who spend their spare time fishing you will soon deduce that worthwhile results may lie in wait. The best advice is to watch what they do and go where they go. Inexpensive tackle is available. Los Lobos Island off Fuerteventura is one of the best locations. Deep-sea fishing charters for the likes of shark, barracuda, marlin, and tuna are available from Los Cristianos (Tenerife), Puerto de Mogán (Gran Canaria), Playa Blanca (Lanzarote), and Corralejo (Fuerteventura).

Golf: The following are 18-hole championship-standard golf courses:

Gran Canaria: Real Club de Golf de Las Palmas — without doubt the most scenic course in the Canaries and also the oldest in all Spain, with a formidable roll-call of great modern golfers; Campo de Golf, Maspalomas.

Tenerife: Amarilla Golf and Country Club and Golf del Sur — both near Los Abrigos; Real Golf Club de Tenerife, La Laguna; Club de Golf El Péñon, Guamasa.

Lanzarote: Club de Golf de Costa Teguise.

Horseback-riding: There are stables with instructors at a number of locations:

Gran Canaria: Club Bandama, Rancho Park, Picadero del Oasis, and El Alamo, all at Playa del Inglés/Maspalomas.

Tenerife: Cuadra Los Orovales, Puerto de la Cruz; Amarilla Golf Club Riding Centre, near Los Abrigos.

Mountain biking: Mountain bikes can be hired without any problems at most major resorts.

Parachuting: If you have never tried parachuting before you may never find a softer place to land than on the sand dunes of Maspalomas. Contact the Aéroclub Maspalomas (tel. 76 24 47) for details.

Tennis: Most *urbanizaciones* and large hotels have their own courts. Public courts are few and far between.

Walking: All the islands except Fuerteventura and Lanzarote are good for serious walkers. Guided walks and special trails are mapped out for those intending to walk Mount Teide on Tenerife, and local tourist information offices may be able to help with trails in other National Parks.

WATER SPORTS

Scuba diving: Look in the important watersport centres such as Playa de las Américas (Tenerife), Puerto Rico (Gran Canaria), Corralejo (Fuerteventura), and Puerto del Carmen and Costa Teguise (Lanzarote). Try also Los Gigantes and Las Galletas (both Tenerife).

Surfing: A few beaches have the right conditions for surfing. Playa de Martiánez at Puerto de la Cruz (Tenerife) is very popular and you can also ride the waves at Playa de las Canteras, Las Palmas (Gran Canaria).

Swimming: There are many safe family beaches at all the major resorts, where breakwaters have created lagoon-like conditions. Be careful at all times on all other beaches. Even seemingly calm waters can hide dangerous undertows.

*Splash into one of the Canaries' many
pristine swimming spots.*

Never swim alone. Some of the popular beaches have life-guards and many now use a flag system: red — don't swim; yellow — swim with caution; green — safe to swim.

Water-skiing: This is less popular than windsurfing in the Canaries but is still usually available at all the major watersport resorts (see Scuba diving). Jet-skiing is also widely available.

Windsurfing: The Canaries are a windsurfer's delight, particularly for the more experienced. Fuerteventura is the mecca. The winds at Sotavento Beach at Jandía regularly blow force 5–9 and in July the world championships are held here. All levels are catered for at the centres listed under Scuba diving (see above). Other recommended places include most resorts on Fuerteventura and on El Médano (Tenerife).

Yachting: You will find the best *Club Náuticos* at Las Palmas and Puerto Rico (Gran Canaria), Santa Cruz (Tenerife), and El Castillo/Caleta de Fustes (Fuerteventura).

SPECTATOR SPORTS

Canaries wrestling *(lucha canaria):* Rather like sumo wrestling, *lucha canaria* is a mixture of civilized ritual and caveman huffing and puffing. The basic aim is to throw the other man to the ground. The roots of the sport are hard to trace. Some say it came from Egypt, while others believe the Guanches may have devised it.

Fiestas and folklore exhibitions are still the tourist's best chance of seeing *la lucha*. Bouts are also held regularly at the Lopez Socas Stadium in Las Palmas between December and May, and at the Tigaiga Hotel, Puerto de la Cruz, every Sunday morning. Otherwise, check in the local press

Vela Latina: *Lateens*, old-fashioned Canaries sailing rigs with triangular sails, race against each other on Saturday afternoons and Sunday mornings at Las Palmas and Puerto Rico, Gran Canaria, between April and September.

Folk music of the Canaries combines the spirits of Spain and South America.

OTHER ACTIVITIES

Folklore

The folk music of the Canaries stands as a reminder that the archipelago has always been a bridge between Spain and the New World. While most local songs sound Spanish, others would be perfectly at home in South America. Many can be traced far back into the islands' history.

Folk music is usually played by quite large groups of young and old musicians, and includes boleros, fandangos, tangos, and other vaguely familiar rhythms. The instruments are guitars and *timples* (small stringed instruments like ukuleles), drums, and flutes. Some songs are known and sung on all the islands; others have a local flavour.

Folklore shows are regularly featured in all the tourist centres, though by definition these are somewhat artificial. The only time you will see folklore staged for local people is at a fiesta.

Festivals

What with saints' days, religious and public holidays, village feast days, and two solid weeks of *Carnaval* you would be very unlucky to visit the islands, particularly in the summer, and not catch some festivity or other. Here are a few of the most colourful events:

January: *Cabalgata de los Reyes* (Procession of the Three Kings): costumes, brass bands, camel cavalcades. Gran Canaria (Las Palmas), Tenerife (Santa Cruz, Garachico), Gomera (Valle Gran Rey).

February/March: *Carnaval*: winter opera and music festival (see below). Gran Canaria (Las Palmas), Tenerife (Santa Cruz).

Fiesta de Nuestra Señora de la Candelaria: Lanzarote (La Oliva).

Revelers pull out all the stops when dressing up for **Carnaval.**

Carnaval de Nuestra Señora del Rosario: festival of music and dance plus Canarian wrestling. Lanzarote (Puerto del Rosario).

March/April: *Semana Santa* (Holy Week): solemn pre-Easter processions in many towns and cities throughout the islands.

Commemoration of the Incorporation of the Islands under the Crown of Castille. Gran Canaria (Las Palmas).

April/May: *Festivales de España:* traditional theatre, ballet, music, and general arts. Gran Canaria (Las Palmas), Tenerife (Santa Cruz).

May: spring festivals, opera. Tenerife (Santa Cruz).

Fiestas de la Cruz: processions, festivities, and fireworks. All places with Cruz (cross) in their name.

May/June: Fiestas de Corpus Christi: see below.

June: *Romería de San Isidro*: procession of ox-drawn carts laden with local produce. Tenerife (La Orotava).

Fiestas de San Juan (Feast of St. John): bonfires and ancient festivities. Tenerife (Icod de los Vinos).

July: *Romería de San Benito:* procession of ox-drawn carts laden with local produce. Tenerife (La Laguna).

Fiestas del Mar (Festival of the Sea): water sports and activities and religious ceremonies combined. Tenerife (Santa Cruz, Puerto de la Cruz).

Fiesta de San Buenaventura: important local festival featuring Canarian wrestling. Fuerteventura (Betancuria).

Fiesta de la Virgen del Carmen: a celebration of Our Lady of Carmen Virgin, the patron saint of all seamen. All islands, any village or town by the sea.

Romerías de Santiago Apóstol (Festival of St. James): pilgrimage, fireworks. Gran Canaria (Gáldar, San Bartolomé), Tenerife (Santa Cruz).

August: *Fiesta de Nuestra Señora de las Nieves* (Our Lady of the Snows): an interesting mixture of religious piety and general fun and games. Gran Canaria (Agaete), La Palma (several locations).

Fiesta de la Asunción (Assumption): re-enactment of the appearance of the Blessed Virgin to the Guanches. Tenerife (Candelaria).

Burial of the Sardine

Of all the island festivities, Burial of the Sardine (held during *Carnaval*) is surely the most bizarre. A huge board and timber sardine of *Jaws* proportions is hauled solemnly on a large float from an appointed place to the sea. Accompanying it are hundreds of "mourners" making the most incredible din with their mock anguish, weeping and wailing in the wake of the "deceased" fish. Beauty queens, transvestites-for-the-night, and whole families dressed in stylized black mourning gear make up a completely surreal funeral party.

At the sea the sardine is ritually burned and a great firework display is given.

Fiestas de San Ginés: concerts, competitions, fireworks, and a camel parade. Lanzarote (Arrecife).

Bajada de la Rama (Descent of the Branch): an ancient Guanche ceremony invoking rain. Gran Canaria (Agaete).

September: *Semana Colón* (Christopher Columbus Week): Gomera (San Sebastián).

Romería de la Virgen del Pino: religious festivities celebrating Our Lady of the Pine. Gran Canaria (Teror).

Fiestas del Santísimo Cristo: floats, flowers, and fireworks, processions, sports, classical theatre, and poetry readings. Tenerife (La Laguna, Tacaronte).

Fiesta de la Virgen de la Peña: island-wide celebrations of the patron saint of Fuerteventura. Pilgrimage to Vega del Rio de Palma, near Betancuria.

Fiesta de la Virgen de los Volcanes: a celebration of a miraculous deliverance from volcanic destruction. Lanzarote (Mancha Blanca, Tinajo)

October: *Fiesta de Nuestra Señora de la Luz*: flowers, fireworks and a maritime procession. Gran Canaria (Las Palmas).

November: *Fiesta del Rancho de Animas*: revival of ancient folklore. Gran Canaria (Teror).

December: *Fiesta de Santa Lucía* (The Festival of Lights): Lanzarote (Máguez, near Haria), Gran Canaria (Arucas, Gáldar, Santa Lucia).

Carnaval

For ten days each year, *Carnaval* is the time when thousands of Canarios celebrate the spring. Shops and businesses close and young and old flood the streets in fancy dress, dancing to pulsating Latin rhythms.

Villages and groups of one kind or another dress according to chosen themes, with magnificent and often outrageous costumes that can take a whole year to put together. Bands and dancers mingle with floats, tourists are treated with good-natured humour, and many don masks and costumes to join in the fun. The music and dancing continue until late, with parties everywhere.

Carnaval is biggest and best in Santa Cruz and Puerto de la Cruz in Tenerife and in Las Palmas on Gran Canaria, where it has all the razzmatazz of Rio's Carnaval and the Mardi Gras of New Orleans. Visitors come from all over Europe and Spain for these events, and hotels are often full, so book well ahead if you plan to visit at this time of year.

Corpus Christi

After *Carnaval*, this is the most spectacular celebration on the islands, though it is of a completely different nature.

As an act of devotion at this religious time, coloured volcanic sand, coloured salt, or flower petals are painstakingly arranged on central paved areas to make up enormous artworks in the form of either elaborate abstract patterns or religious pictures, possibly copied from an Old Master. The most extravagant are to be seen in La Orotava and La Laguna on Tenerife, but Las Palmas on Gran Canaria and many other

Not everyone enjoys Carnaval!

towns and villages throughout the islands also participate.
The pictures are ruined, sometimes in a matter of moments,
by the feet of the ensuing procession and certainly by the
first rainfall. Only photographs preserve the memory of
months of hard work.

Colourful fiestas of song and dance, food and wine, known
as *Romerías,* follow hard on the heels of Corpus Christi to re-
dress the sobriety.

Flamenco

Moorish in its presumed origins, flamenco bears a striking
resemblance to the wailing chants of Arab music. The shows in
the Canaries are popular tourist attractions.

There are two main types of flamenco song: one, bouncy
and cheerful is known as *cante chico*; the other, *cante jondo,*
deals with all human tragedy and is performed in the slow,
piercing, melodramatic style of the great flamenco artists.
Predictably you will hear more *cante chico* at the *tablao*
(floorshow) in the Canaries than *cante jondo.*

Flamenco evenings are staged by all the large hotels but
the best place to catch one is in a small, smoky bar or restaurant in town where you can hear the rustle of the dancer's
swirling dress and feel much more a part of the dramatic action. Troupes move from bar to bar and are usually advertised in advance.

A variation on the theme is a floorshow sometimes termed
"Spanish ballet." This is a hybrid of ballet, flamenco and folk
dancing accompanied by local and classic Spanish tunes.

FOR CHILDREN

With almost guaranteed sunshine, soft sandy beaches, and
lots of amusements options off the beach, the more popular
Canary islands are perfect for children. Many hotels have

special features for the young, ranging from poolside games to babysitters. When the appeal of swimming and sand castles begins to wane, consider some of the following:

Ride a camel. In Lanzarote a dromedary (one hump, not two) will take you on a 20-minute trip up and down one of the "Fire Mountains." Two riders are accommodated at a time, slung on yoked seats on either side of the camel's neck, so it's a great adventure for two children. You will also find dromedaries for hire on Gran Canaria and Tenerife.

Go go-karting. There are tracks at Maspalomas (Gran Canaria) and Playa de las Américas (Tenerife). The karts never travel too quickly and are so low to the ground that they can't tip over. However, being so low they also give a thrilling sensation of speed, and your only problem will be getting your child off when it's time to go. Adult drivers are usually welcome too.

Go sailing. There are trips on beautiful old restored sailing ships and memorable whale and dolphin safaris from Los Cristianos, spotting pilot whales and friendly porpoises. However, do be aware that some of these trips can be too long for younger children.

Older children may like to take the plunge and learn windsurfing. There is no shortage of instructors and it's as easy as falling off a log.

Make a splash. Water parks are becoming quite popular in the islands, and water-babies of all ages can splash happily while parents join in or simply sunbathe. If you really want to keep the children occupied, ask them to tell you how the baffling bright orange "tap in the sky" *trompe l'oeil* at Aguapark Octopus (Playa de las Américas, Tenerife) works!

Pick a banana. A trip to the banana plantation of Bananera El Guanche (see pages 24), outside Puerto de la Cruz, Tenerife, may not initially sound very exciting to a youngster, but the sight of whole banana fists growing wild is a novelty and the easy-to-follow video that precedes the self-guided tour makes learning fun. Adults get a banana liqueur at the end of the tour.

Watch the birdie (and the dolphins). Choose from Tenerife's Loro Park, Gran Canaria's Palmitos Park, or Lanzarote's Guinate Tropical Park to see hilarious bird shows and beautiful feathered creatures from all over the world. At Loro Park there is also a dolphinarium and the new Thai village.

Cowboys and Indians. Gran Canaria's Sioux City is a film set come to life, with plenty of American Western surprises transferred quite effortlessly to the mid-Atlantic. Go along for an evening show and barbecue (see page 41).

Meet the Guanches. Older children are sure to be fascinated by the Guanche skulls, skeletons, and mummies kept at both the Museo Canario in Las Palmas and the Museo Arqueológico at Santa Cruz on Tenerife.

¡Carnaval! Children who enjoy dressing up will love *Carnaval.* It is often the children who get the best costumes anyway.

Unless you are an expert at making your own entertainment, children probably *won't* enjoy Gomera, La Palma or El Hierro. There isn't much for them in Fuerteventura either, aside from Corralejo.

SHOPPING

In 1852 the Canary Islands were declared a duty-free zone in order to stimulate the development of the archipelago and its ports as an Atlantic staging base. The plan worked,

A chemist's is called *farrmacia* (fahrmahthyah), and they don't sell books, film, or newspapers.

and the islands still boast some of the largest, busiest seaports in the whole of Spain.

In recent years the duty-free zone has been transformed into a trade-free zone, into which goods are imported without restrictions from all over the world and the luxury tax is lower than in most countries.

Many shops in the main resorts stock cameras, calculators, watches, perfume, jewellery, leather goods, spirits, and tobacco — in fact all the things that you can buy in airport duty-free shops. Aside from spirits and local tobacco, however, there are few real bargains.

Shopping Hours

Most stores in the Canaries maintain Spanish-style siesta-led opening hours. They open around 9:00 A.M. and close for lunch at 1:00 P.M. They re-open at 4 or 5:00 P.M. and close for the day at 7 or 8:00 P.M. In the busier tourist resorts a few shops are open later into the evening, especially at the height of the season. Department stores are open between 10:00 A.M. and 8:00 P.M.

Best Buys

Best buys in the Canaries should in theory be those items that carry a luxury tax at home, which usually means electronic goods, cameras, etc. However, for Europeans and North Americans, there are few bargains. Worse still, there are now many Far East fakes in the Canaries.

Spirits and tobacco are the best bargains. Local brands of spirits are the cheapest, though rarely of high quality, and most international brands are also bargains. Local cigarettes are fairly rough but cigar smokers can find both price and quality. The cigars of La Palma in particular draw high praise.

For the really keen shopper, uncut gems, silver jewellery, silks, leatherware, and furs may be of interest.

Indian Bazaars

Many of the shops selling luxury goods in the Canaries are owned by Indian entrepreneurs. Generally prices are flexible and haggling is accepted as part of the shopping process. You may assume that this is the case in any shop where prices are not marked.

Mercados

The most colourful shopping opportunities in the Canaries are at the open-air markets usually held on a Sunday morning. The Sunday morning *rastro* (flea market) near the port in Las Palmas is particularly good, and the Mercado de Nuestra Señora de Africa at Santa Cruz de Tenerife is recommended at any time.

Signs: *revajas* **are items on sale.**

Many provincial towns and villages hold weekly Sunday markets where haggling is, of course, all part of the fun.

Island Products

The most celebrated local handicraft is embroidery. Many tourist excursions visit craft workshops where local girls are engaged in delicate needlework on bedspreads, towels, and

Cigar smokers will be pleased with both price and quality of the local products.

napkins and lacemakers work on doilies, tablecloths, and other items. The beauty of these places is that you can see what you are getting. Your purchase will also help keep the island's unique craft industry alive. Do not expect great bargains, however. If you are offered lace or embroidery cheap in the street it was probably made on a machine in the Far East.

Pottery is another possibility, albeit a rather more weighty one. There are several charmingly primitive styles practised in the Canaries.

Centras artesanìas is a small chain of state-subsidised crafts shops in Tenerife selling pottery, wood carvings, jewellery, and paintings.

Last-Day Special

A few days before you are due to fly home, order some *strelitzias* — Bird of Paradise flowers. Compared with the price of exotic

Good times — drinks are cheap and plentiful throughout the Canaries.

flora elsewhere these really are a bargain, even when packed into an air-freight box which makes them very easy to transport home.

NIGHTLIFE

In the main tourist centres of the Canaries you can find almost any style of nightlife you require, from extravagant and formal floorshows to cheap and rowdy karaoke bars.

Young at Heart

All the large resorts and quite a few of the developing ones cater to tourists at the younger end of the market who basically want to drink large quantities of cheap alcohol and meet fellow tourists in bars and discos. Admittance is free in most music bars, video bars and karaoke bars, but discos charge a small entrance fee that includes the first drink.

Cabaret

Most of the large resorts boast a major cabaret attraction. One of the biggest and probably the best is the **Son a Mar** at San Agustín (near Maspalomas) on Gran Canaria. A blend of Paris, Las Vegas, Brazil, and Hollywood by night, it features high-kicking showgirls, and song and dance on a grand scale. A more informal night out can be had at nearby **Sioux City**, where you can enjoy a Wild West barbecue (see page 41).

Tenerife is predictably well served by a number of lavish venues. Entertainment at the **Tenerife Palace** in Puerto de la Cruz is in a similar vein to that at the Son a Mar. A few miles outside Puerto is **La Cueva**, an old Guanche dwelling that now hosts topless African dancers and a Hawaiian show. In the south of the island is the **Castillo San Miguel,** which stages medieval-style banquets complete with jousting knights.

Lanzarote is much quieter than the "big two." **Bavarian Dancing** at Puerto del Carmen and **Moonlight Bay,** nearby, are the main international cabaret venues.

More unusual nightspot venues include two of César Manrique's creations: the Lido Martiánez at Puerto de la Cruz becomes the **Andromeda** night club after dark, and on Lanzarote the **Jameos del Agua** hosts folklore shows and a disco.

Gambling

There are two main casinos in the islands. The landmark **Casino Taoro** at Puerto de la Cruz is the most famous in betting circles, the other is the **Casino Tamarindos Gran Canaria**, at the Hotel Meliá Tamarindos San Agustín (which also stages the Son a Mar). Similar games are played in both — French and American roulette, blackjack and craps. The minimum stake is from 200–500 pesetas, though slot machines cater for tighter budgets.

A modest entrance fee is charged, and you will need your passport for security purposes. It is fascinating just watching the monied clientele in these places, not to mention the lightning reflexes of the croupiers, particularly as they scoop away the unfortunate punters' gaming chips. The safest rule for amateurs is to decide in advance how much you can afford to lose (which you probably will) and stick rigidly to it.

Concerts, Opera, Ballet

Highbrow or cultural evening entertainment is not always well advertised, but it certainly exists, and notices can be found in the Spanish papers a day or two before the event. Each provincial capital boasts its own 19th-century opera house.

In Santa Cruz the **Teatro Guimerá** is strong on opera. It is also home to the Tenerife Symphony Orchestra, whose season runs from September to May or June.

The **Teatro Pérez Galdós** in Las Palmas has decorations by Néstor de la Torre (see page 38). Opera, *zarzuela* (Spanish musical comedy), ballet, and symphony concerts are held here.

EATING OUT

Travellers who treat local food and drink as an integral part of their holiday enjoyment will rarely be disappointed in the Canaries. There are some excellent Spanish restaurants in the islands, and cosmopolitan cuisine as elaborate or as downbeat as you please also thrives. You can choose to be served in candle-lit continental luxury or simply go to the nearest fast-food outlet.

> **Male waiters are called** *camarero* **(cahmahrayro),** **female** *camarera* **(cahmahrayrah).**

If you want to sample real Canarian food look for the name *tipico*, which indicates a good-value, often country-style restaurant serving fresh local food.

Local cooking is colourful and often spicy.

Restaurants

Throughout Spain and the Canaries restaurants are officially graded by a "fork" system. One fork is the lowest grade, five forks is the elite. However, these ratings are awarded according to the facilities and the degree of luxury that the restaurant offers, not the quality of the food. Five forks will therefore guarantee a hefty bill but not necessarily the finest food. Some of the best restaurants in the islands have fewer than five forks because their owners give priority to the quality of the food and wine rather than the standard of the furnishings.

A selection of recommended restaurants is enclosed at the end of this guide. However, if in doubt, don't forget the universal criterion for sizing up a restaurant. Are the locals eating there?

All Spanish restaurants should offer a *menú del dia* (daily special). This is normally three courses, including wine, at a very reasonable set price. If the waiter asks you "*¿Menú?*," he means, "Do you wish to order the *menú del dia?*" If you want to read the menu, ask for "*La carta, por favor.*"

In all restaurants the prices on the menu include taxes and a service charge, but it is customary to leave a tip if you are served efficiently and cheerily. Five percent is acceptable, 10

Jamón Serrano

A leg of *jamón serrano* is a standard fixture in many Spanish restaurants and in nearly all *tapas* bars. The name means "mountain ham" and is often abbreviated simply to *serrano*. A *tapa*-sized portion comprises several wafer-thin slices on dry bread. The ham in use sits on a special holder horizontally behind the bar while others hang vertically from the ceiling. A small cup often hangs below to catch any juices. The hams are cured in the mountains of mainland Spain, the best coming from Huelva in Andalusia. You can gauge from the cost of a few thin slices that each leg represents a sizeable investment. When all the best meat has gone from the bone the leg is used for stewing or soup.

percent is generous. Never eat in a restaurant that does not display prices. You will almost always be guaranteed an unpleasant shock at the end of your meal. Also, remember to work out in advance how much your bill will be when ordering fish priced by the kilo.

Mealtimes are generally not as late in the Canaries as on the Spanish mainland. The peak hours are after 1:00 P.M. for lunch and after 8:00 P.M. for dinner, but you can get a meal in many places at just about any time of day.

Bars and Cafés

From sunrise to the middle of the night, from the first coffee to the last brandy, the café is a very special institution in daily life in the Ca-

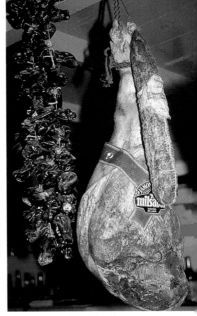

Hanging hams —
jamòn serrano *are*
ubiquitous in tapas bars.

naries. In practice there is little difference between a bar and a café, apart from the bias of the bar towards alcoholic drink.

Most bars are noisy places, in keeping with the general decibel level in Spain. The ubiquitous TV is almost always switched on, a radio or tape may well be playing simultaneously, and the infuriating gaming machine in the corner

Signs:
Smoker—
fumadores
Nonsmoker—
no fumadores

pumps out in electronic staccato tones the first few bars to "Colonel Bogey" as the locals try to hit the jackpot.

Bars and cafés are the meeting places for both locals and tourists, to swap the day's news in pidgin English, Spanish, or German or to shout at the TV screen whenever the football is on. The price of a cup of coffee buys you a ringside seat for as long as you care to stay; no one will rush you to leave or to buy another drink.

Wines and spirits are served at all hours everywhere in Spain, so don't raise an eyebrow when you see a local knocking back a large measure of colourless firewater first thing in the morning. You may also be surprised to see that children frequent bars with impunity. The Spanish consider this quite natural, even late at night.

Like restaurants, bars and cafés usually include a service charge, but an additional small tip is the custom if you have spent any length of time in the establishment. Prices are 10–15 percent lower if you stand or sit at the bar rather than occupy a table.

Tapas

A *tapa* is a small portion of food served in a bar to encourage you to keep drinking instead of heading off to a restaurant for a meal. The word *tapa* means "lid" and comes from the custom of giving a free bite of food with a drink, the food served on a saucer atop the glass like a lid. Nowadays it is rare to see *tapas* given away, but *tapas* bars are more popular than ever.

Bona fide *tapas* bars, and indeed many simple bars, have a whole counter display of hot and cold snacks which makes choosing very easy. Just point to the one you like. Some of the most common Canarian (and Spanish) *tapas* are olives, meat-

Dining out is likely to be a double pleasure featuring both fabulous food and lively entertainment.

> **Enjoy your meal! -
> Buen provecho!**
> (*Bwayn provaychoh*)

balls, Russian salad, local cheese, wedges of Spanish omelette (*tortilla*), *chorizo* (spicy salami-style sausage), octopus salad, prawns with garlic dressing, mushrooms, deep fried crabmeat, and mountain-cured ham (*jamón serrano*).

Tapas are always accompanied by a small basket of fresh bread. This is often lightly flavoured with caraway and is delicious.

Portion control: *una tapa* is the smallest amount; *una ración* is half a small plateful and *una porción* is getting towards a meal in itself. Keep your enthusiasm to try everything on your first day in check. It is quite easy to spend more on *tapas* than on a good restaurant meal.

Breakfast

For Spaniards this is the least significant meal of the day. A coffee with a *tostado* (piece of toast) or a pastry is about the size of it. Down by the port you may well find the fishermen breakfasting on *calamares* (lightly battered squid), which is surprisingly delicious first thing in the morning. If you have a sweet tooth look for a place selling *churros*. These are deep-fried batter fritters, sugared and then traditionally dunked in coffee or hot chocolate.

Most hotels offer huge breakfast buffets, including a truly international array of cereals, juices, dried and fresh fruits, cold meats and cheeses, plus bacon and eggs. Many cafés also cater to tourists by offering a *desayuno completo* of orange juice, bacon, eggs, toast, and coffee.

Canaries Cuisine

The local cooking is usually wholesome, filling, and delicious. Unfortunately for those in search of the real thing it is often much easier to find a "real British pub" than a *tipico*. When you do, look for the following:

Rancho canario — a rich meat and vegetable soup thickened with *gofio*, the Canarian staff of life. *Gofio* was first eaten by the prehistoric Guanches. It used to be made of crushed barley or rye but now it is usually wholemeal or maize meal, toasted and milled.

Garbanzo compuesto — chick-pea stew with potatoes, also with *gofio*.

Puchero — a stew of meat (usually pork or veal) and vegetables.

Potaje — a rich, thick vegetable soup.

All of the above are served as starters but for lesser appetites are meals in themselves.

Papas viudas (literally "widow potatoes") — roast potatoes with carrots, peas, parsley, olives, green pepper, ham, and onions.

Malvasía wine in a bodega.

Sancocho — a stew of salted fish (usually sea bass or salt cod) with sweet potatoes, vegetables, and *mojo picón* (see page 98).

Conejo en salmorejo — rabbit in a spicy sauce made with *mojo picón* (see below).

Papas arrugadas (literally wrinkled potatoes) — potatoes baked in their skins in very salty water, rolled in rock salt, and generally served with *mojo picón*.

Mojo picón — a red piquant sauce composed mainly of paprika and chilli. It is often spicy, so approach cautiously.

Mojo verde — by contrast, a cool green herb sauce usually made of coriander and parsley. An excellent side to grilled fish.

Surrounded by the Atlantic Ocean, the Canarians naturally consider fish a vital part of their diet. You will find most kinds of seafood here, from octopus to swordfish and local varieties such as *vieja* ("widow" fish) and *cherna* (a type of grouper). Don't underestimate the humble sardine; plump and juicy, they are delicious straight off the barbecue or grill (*a la parilla*).

Meat is just as common on most menus, even though much of it is imported from mainland Spain or South America. Prices are very reasonable and the quality is usually good.

Goat's-milk cheeses vary from island to island and are certainly worth trying. You will also see *Manchego*, a famous hard, unpasteurized cheese from the mainland.

Canarians do not go in for desserts much, but do look for *bien me sabe* ("How good it tastes"), a confection of honey, almonds, and rum. Cakes and pastries are best sampled in a *dulcería*, a cross between a tea-room and an ordinary café. El Hierro is noted for its *quesadilla*, a fluffy cake made with lemon and cheese, though quite unlike a conventional cheesecake.

Spanish Cuisine

Since the Canaries are Spanish and a good number of tourists are from Spain there are some excellent Spanish restaurants on the islands. Look for these specialities:

Gazpacho — a chilled soup made from tomatoes, peppers, cucumbers and garlic, served with various crudités.

Sopa de ajo — a thick soup of chopped garlic, with paprika, breadcrumbs, and eggs.

Huevos a la flamenca — baked eggs, asparagus, red pepper, and peas atop a sausage-and-ham base.

Paella — Spain's most famous dish is named after the large, black iron pan in which it is cooked. Ingredients vary, but it is basically rice cooked in stock, flavoured and coloured with saffron, plus a mixture of chicken or rabbit, fish, shellfish, sausage, pork, and peppers.

Alcoholic Drinks

In Elizabethan times Canaries wine was served at all the top tables in Europe. Tastes may have changed, but the local wines are still very good. Unfair as it may seem, local wines are dearer than table wines imported from the mainland because they are made on a much smaller scale.

> **In Shakespears's days *sherry wine* was called *sack* or *sherries sack*. Sack derived from the Spanish word "sacar" (to export), while *sherries* comes from the name of the town *Jerez*, where this wine originated.**

Several of the wines originate from the volcanic soil and this gives them a rich, full flavour. Historically, Canaries wines were of the Malmsey (*malvasía*) variety. These tend to be very sweet but there are drier varieties that retain the same rich, distinctive bouquet. You are more likely to be offered local wines in country restaurants than in the big resorts.

Rum (*ron*) may conjure up visions of the Caribbean, but it is also made in the Canaries and is very popular here. It is often mixed with cola in a *Cuba libre*. A liqueur called *ron-miel* (literally rum honey) is a speciality of Gomera.

Local distilleries also produce fruit-based liqueurs, particularly banana, but also orange and other tropical flavours.

Sangría is probably the most popular tourist drink throughout Spain. It is a mixture of red wine, orange and lemon juices, brandy, and mineral water topped with lots of sliced fruit and ice. This perfect hot-weather concoction can pack quite a punch.

Sherry *(Jerez)*, that most famous of Spanish drinks, is not so popular in the Canaries as it is on the mainland but, together with Spanish brandy (colloquially known as *coñac*), Spanish-style champagne *(cava)*, and a whole host of international brand names, it is available in all good bars, served in huge devil-may-care measures.

Supermarket shelves are full of the same names at eye-popping prices and are always much cheaper than airport duty-free shops.

Canarian beer *(cerveza)* is usually Tropical or Dorada lager. The latter is recommended. Beer is served either draft or in bottles measuring one-third of a litre. Draft measures vary but basically if you want a small beer ask for *"una cerveza pequeña."* *"Una cerveza grande"* is about the same size as a British pint. Remember that Spanish lager is 50 per cent stronger than standard British lager.

Tea, Coffee, and Soft Drinks

The Spanish usually drink coffee *(café)* as opposed to tea *(té)*. This can be either *solo* (small and black), *con leche* (a large cup made with milk, often in a frothy cappuccino-style), or *cortado* (a small cup with a little milk). It is strong and very tasty. Mineral water *(agua mineral)* is either sparkling *(agua con gas)* or still *(agua sin gas)*. Ice-cream parlours sell *granizado*, slushy iced fruit juice in several flavours, and freshly pressed orange juice *(zumo de naranjas)*, the latter being surprisingly expensive.

INDEX

Where there is more than one set of page references, main entries are in bold type.

accommodation 7, 42, 82
Agaete *36*, **44**, 81
Aguapark Octopus 33, 84
alcoholic drinks 16, 25, **99–100**
Arguineguín 42
Arrecife **48**, 81
Arucas 43

Bajamar 26
ballets 90-91
Bananera El Guanche **24**, 84
Barlovento 70
Barranco de Guyadeque 47
Barranco del Infierno 18
bars 89
Basilica Nuestra Señora del Pino 46
Betancuria **59**, *59*, 81
Botánico, Jardín 24

cabarets 89–90
Cactus, Jardín de 54
Cactus Park 33
cafés 93-95
Caldera de Bandama 47
Caldera de Taburiente 68
Caleta de Fustes **58**, 76
camel rides 51, 84
canaries (birds) 40
Canaries wrestling 76
Candelaria **30**, 80
Carnaval *79*, *82*, **81–82**, 85
Casino Taoro 54, 90
Castillo de San Gabriel 48
Castillo de San José 48
Castillo de San Miguel **33–34**, 89

Castillo de Santa Bárbara 54
cathedrals (catedrals) **25**, 43
caves 13, 43-44, 55
childrens' activities 83-85
churches (iglesias) 21, 23, 25-26, 43, 48, 60, 63, 67
Colombus, Christopher 14, **38–39**, 62-63
concerts 90
Corpus Christi 27, **82**
Corralejo 57
Costa Calma 60, *61*
Costa Teguise 54
crafts 27, 53-54, 87-88
Cristo de los Dolores 25-26
Cruz de Tejeda 45
cuevas see caves
cuisine 97-99

Degollada de Peraza 65
Drago Milenaro (Dragon Tree) *32*, 33
drinks 16, 25, 99-100

eating out 91–100
El Abrigo 31
El Castillo 58
El Cotillo 58
El Golfo (El Hierro) 71-72
El Golfo (Lanzarote) 49–50
El Hierro 9, 14, 18, **70–72**, *72*
El Sabinal 72
Ermita de San Antonio Abad 38

festivals 78–81
fishing 73

flamenco 83
folklore shows 38, 54, 57, 78
food and drink 16, 25, 91–100
Franco, Francisco 18, 22
Fuerteventura 7, 9, 14, 18, **56–61**, 75, 76

gambling 90
Garachico **33–34**, 78
Garajonay National Park 64–5
go-karting 33
golf 73
Gomera 7, 9, 14, 18, **61–66**
Graciosa 55
Gran Canaria 7, 9, 14, **34–47**
Guanches **12–13**, 14, 30, 31, 44, 70, 85
Guía 44
Guinate Tropical Park 55

Haría 55
history 10–18
Horseback-riding 73
hotels 9, 71

Jameos del Agua **54–55**, 90
Jandía 60, 76

La Esperanza 18, 28
La Geria 52
La Laguna **25**, 27, 73, 80, 82,
La Oliva **58**, 78
La Orotava **26**, 79, 82
La Palma 7, 9, 12, 18, **66-70**, 80, 86
Lago Martiánez 22, *23*
Lanzarote 7, 9, 14, *15*, **47–56**, *56*,73, 75, 78, 79, 81, 85, 90
Las Cañadas National Park 28
Las Nieves 68
Las Palmas 12, 17, **35–39**, *41*,
79, 81, 82, 85, 87, 90
Las Teresitas 22
Loro Parque 24
Los Berrazales 44
Los Cristianos 31, 73
Los Gigantes 34, 75
Los Lobos, Isla de 58, 73
Los Organos 65
Los Roques *10*, 30
Los Telares 64

Manrique, César 22, 49, **50**, 52, 54–55
Masca 34
Maspalomas **40–41**, *53*, 73, 84
Mazo 70
Mercedes, Monte de las 26
Mesón de la Silla 45–46
Mirador de la Peña 72
Mirador del Río 55
Mirador del Time 69
Mirador las Cumbres 28
Montaña Tropical 49
Montañas del Fuego 51
Monumento al Campesino 52
Morro del Jable 61
mountain biking 75
Moya 43
museums 12, 20–21, 26, 39, 46, 49, 54, 60

naturist beaches 40-41, 50
Nelson, Horatio 16, 21, 40, **89-90**
nightlife 34

operas 90
Orotava Valley **27**, 28
Orzola 55

Pájara 60

Palacio de Carta 21
Palmitos Parque 41, *42*
Papagayo (parrot) beaches 50
parachuting 75
paradors 30, 45, 63, 72
Playa Blanca 50, 73
Playa de las Américas 18, **31–32**, 75, 84
Playa de las Canteras **36**, 75
Playa de Martiánez 22, 75
Playa de Sotavento 60
Playa del Inglés **40**, 73
Pueblo Canario 38
Puerto de la Cruz 8, 19, **22–25**, 75, 80, 82, 89, 90
Puerto de las Nieves 44
Puerto de Mogán 42, 73
Puerto de Santiago 34
Puerto de Tazacorte 69
Puerto del Carmen 49
Puerto Pesquero 22
Puerto Rico 42, 75, 76
Punta de Teno 34

Reptilandia 44
restaurants 37, 40, 49, 61, 72, **92-93** see also *paradors*
Roque de los Muchachos 70
Roque Nublo 45

sailing 43, 77, 84
Salinas de Janubio 49
San Agustín 40, 89
San Sebastian **62-63**, 81
Santa Cruz de la Palma 66-68
Santa Cruz de Tenerife 16, **19-22**, 76, 78, 79, 80, 85
Santuario de Nuestra Señora de las Nieves 68
scuba diving 75
shopping 21, 34, 38, 54, **85-88**

Sioux City 41, 85, 89
sports 73-77
surfing 75
swimming 75-76

Tacoronte **25**, 81
Taganana 26
Tamadaba 46
tapas 95-96
Teguise 53-54
Teide, Mount 8, 19, **28-29**, 75
Tejeda 45
Telde 47
Teneguia (volcano) 69
Tenerife 7, 8, 12-15, **19-34**
tennis 75
Teror 46
Triana 38

Valerón 13, 43
Valle Gran Rey 66
Valverde 71
Vegueta 38
Vela Latina 77
volcanoes 7-8, 47, 50, 51-52, 69

walking 75
water parks 41, 54, **84**
water-skiing 76
watersports 40, 54, **75-76**
windsurfing 54, 57, 60, **76**
wines 16, 25, **99-100**
wrestling, Canaries 76-77

yachting 76

HANDY TRAVEL TIPS

An A–Z Summary of Practical Information

A Accommodation 105
Airports 106
C Camping 106
Car Hire 106
Climate 107
Clothing 107
Complaints 108
Consulates 108
Crime 109
Customs and Entry
Formalities 109
D Disabled
Travellers 110
Driving 111
E Electric Current 113
Emergencies 113
Etiquette 114
G Getting to the Canary
Islands 114
Guides and Tours 115
L Language 115
Lost Property 116
M Maps 116
Medical Care 117

Money Matters 117
N Newspapers and
Magazines 120
O Opening Hours 120
P Photography/Video
121
Police 121
Post Offices 122
Public Holidays 123
Public Transport 123
R Radio and TV 124
Religion 124
Restaurants 124
T Taxis 125
Telephones 125
Time
Differences 125
Tipping 126
Toilets 126
Tourist Information
Offices 126
W Water 127
Y Youth Hostels 127

A

ACCOMMODATION (See also Camping and Youth Hostels.)
Most accommodation in the Canaries is designed for family package
holidays and therefore tends to be of a good medium-high international standard. Aside from hotels there are numerous apartments
and "aparthotels," where each room has its own kitchen facilities yet
retains all the trappings of a hotel. Hotels are government-inspected
and graded 1–5 stars depending upon facilities. Apartments are graded from 1–4 keys.

It is not easy to find cheap accommodation in the major resorts.
You may find the occasional hostal – a modest hotel with an Hs sign
outside (graded 1–3 stars). Pensiones (boarding houses, denoted by
the letter P) are rare, however. Santa Cruz de la Palma is one of the
few places where these are apparent. The letter R, suffixed to a hotel
or hostal sign, indicates residencia. This means that there does not
have to be a restaurant facility and the establishment offers bed and
breakfast only.

The most notable accommodation is found in *Paradores
Nacionales*. These are state-run establishments, sometimes set in
magnificent historic buildings, sometimes in functional modern
blocks. Their common aim is to provide the chance to experience
"the real Spain." All reflect local style, and though they are usually
quite expensive they are nearly always good value. There is a
Parador on all the islands with the exception of Lanzarote (the
Parador on Gran Canaria does not provide accommodation).

When checking in to any accommodation you will be asked to sur-
render your passport for a short period. In general, prices are quoted
per room, not per person.

A selection of hotels can be found in the centre of this guide.

a single/double room	**una habitación sencilla/doble**
with bath/shower	**con baño/ducha**
What's the rate per night?	**Cuál es el precio por noche?**

Canary Islands

AIRPORTS *(aeropuerto)*

All the islands except Gomera have commercial airports. International flights serve Tenerife, Gran Canaria, Lanzarote, and Fuerteventura, while frequent flights shuttle to and from El Hierro and La Palma. Every airport is served by taxis and car-hire companies, and the major airports also have regular bus services.

CAMPING *(camping)*

Official camp sites are rare in the Canaries, although there is nothing to stop you asking private landowners for their permission to pitch a tent. Camping in the National Parks is strictly forbidden.

Nauta Camping/Caravaning at Las Galletas on Tenerife is a well-equipped official site. Gran Canaria has two official sites; Guantámo, by Playa de Tauro near Puerto Rico and Temisas near Agüimes (just west of the airport).

CAR HIRE *(coches de alquiler)*

See also DRIVING. Car hire firms in the Canaries offer a wide range of cars at varying prices. Always shop around for the best deal. Local companies (such as Top-Car Reisen) offer better rates than the multi-national firms. If an advertised rate sounds particularly low, query whether it includes all insurance and taxes. Unlimited mileage is the norm but once again if the price is low, confirm that this is the case.

Third-party insurance is always included but it is worth taking out comprehensive insurance as well. Personal accident insurance may well be covered by your standard travel insurance policy.

You must be over 21 if you are paying by credit card and over 23 if you are paying by cash. In the latter case an additional deposit may be required. Although officially you should have an International Driving Permit, in practice driving licences from all major countries are accepted without question.

I'd like to hire a car.	**Quisiera alquilar un coche.**
for one day/week	**por un día/una semana**

Please include full insurance. **Haga el favor de incluir el seguro a todo riesgo.**

CLIMATE

Despite the popular concept that sunshine is guaranteed here, it is impossible to generalize about the islands. It may be pouring with chilly rain on Gomera or La Palma, while sunbathers bake on Fuerteventura. The mountainous nature of Gran Canaria and the north/south divide of Tenerife mean that the weather can be completely different at opposite ends of each island.

There are two rules of thumb: the easterly islands are drier and warmer than the westerly ones (Lanzarote and Fuerteventura are normally a little warmer than Gran Canaria); the sunnier, warmer weather is likely to be found on the south side of an island.

Be prepared for winds: in spring there is the alisio, a cold and wet gust from the northwest, and in autumn the famous sirocco. Approximate monthly average temperature:

TENERIFE	J	F	M	A	M	J	J	A	S	O	N	D
°C	17	16	17	18	21	22	23	24	23	22	20	18
°F	64	62	64	64	68	71	74	75	74	70	69	64
Rainy days	7	7	5	3	1	0	0	1	2	6	7	6

GRAN CANARIA	J	F	M	A	M	J	J	A	S	O	N	D
°C	17	16	17	17	19	20	22	23	22	22	19	17
°F	62	62	62	64	66	69	72	73	73	71	67	63
Rainy days	8	5	5	3	1	1	1	1	1	5	7	8

CLOTHING

In addition to summer clothes and beach wear don't forget a sweater or jacket for evenings. For excursions to high altitudes you will also need warmer clothing and some sturdy shoes. During the winter some protection from the rain may well come in handy.

Casual wear is the norm, though if you intend to frequent five-star hotels, the best restaurants or the casino, then a jacket and tie (though not obligatory) will not be out of place for men.

Topless bathing has become quite common, though you must cover up off the beach. Shorts and mini-skirts should not be worn when visiting religious places.

COMPLAINTS

By law, all hotels and restaurants must have official complaint forms *(hoja de reclamaciones)* and produce them on demand. The original of this triplicate document should be sent to the Ministry of Tourism; one copy remains with the establishment involved and one copy is given to you. Try to resolve your problem before going through this procedure, as it will be difficult for you to succeed in any claims once you are off the island. However, the very action of asking for the *hoja* may resolve the problem in itself, as tourism authorities take a serious view of malpractice, and can revoke or suspend licences.

You should also inform the local tourist office, or in serious cases the local police, of any complaints and seek their assistance.

In the rare event of a major obstruction, when it is not possible to call in the police, write directly to the Secretaría de Estado de Turismo, Sección de Inspección y Reclamaciones, Duque de Medinaceli, 2, Madrid.

CONSULATES *(consulado)*

Santa Cruz de Tenerife:
British Consulate: Plaza Weyler, 8; tel. 28 68 63

Las Palmas de Gran Canaria:
British Consulate: Edificio Cataluña, Calle de Luis
                                           Morote, 6; tel. 26 25 08/12 16 58

Arrecife de Lanzarote:
British Consul (honorary):   Calle Rubicón, 7; tel. 81 59 28
(10 a.m. to noon only)
US Consulate: Calle Franchy Roca, 5; tel. 27 12 59

Most European countries have consular offices in Santa Cruz and/or Las Palmas.

If you run into trouble with the authorities or the police, contact your consulate for advice.

| Where is the British/American consulate? | ¿Dónde está el consulado británico/americano? |

CRIME

The most common crime against the tourist in the Canaries (as in all Spain) is theft from hire cars. If you park overnight in the street in one of the big towns or resorts, as you may have to, there is every chance that your car will be broken into.

Thieves also operate at certain known tourist locations where cars are left unattended. Never leave anything of value in your car at any time. You should be safe in smaller towns and villages but even here take no chances. The possibility of damaged locks is another good reason why your insurance cover should always be comprehensive.

Hotels recommend that you use the safe deposit box in your room for all valuables, including your passport. However, there is usually a charge for this. Burglaries of holiday apartments do occur, so keep doors and windows locked when you are absent and while you are asleep.

You must report all thefts to the local police within 24 hours for your own insurance purposes, but do not hold out any hope of getting your property back. Petty theft is now so common in some places that the limited police resources are powerless to cope with it.

On a more cheerful note, crimes involving actual violence against tourists are still quite rare in the Canaries.

| I want to report a theft. | **Quiero denunciar un robo.** |

CUSTOMS AND ENTRY FORMALITIES

Most visitors, including citizens of all EU countries, the USA, Canada, Eire, Australia, and New Zealand, require only a valid passport – no visa, no health certificate – to enter Spain. Visitors from South Africa must have a visa. British tourists may no longer enter Spain on a visitor's passport – a full passport is required.

If you expect to remain for longer than 90 days (US citizens 180 days), a Spanish consulate or tourist office can advise you.

Since the Canaries are a free-trade zone, there is no restriction on what you may bring in with you as a tourist. However, it would be absurd to buy duty-free cigarettes or spirits at your airport of departure as you will find the same items much cheaper on the islands.

The following chart shows the main duty-free items that you are allowed to take back into your own country:

Into:	Cigarettes		Cigars		Tobacco	Spirits		Wine
USA	200	or	50 g	or	2,000 g	1 ltr	or	1 ltr
Australia	200	or	250 g	or	250 g	1 ltr	or	`1 ltr
Canada	200	and	50 g	and	900 g	1.1 ltr	or	1.1 ltr
Eire	200	or	50 g	or	250 g	1 ltr	and	2 ltr
N. Zealand	200	or	50 g	or	250 g	1 ltr	and	4.5 ltr
S. Africa	400	and	50 g	and	250 g	1 ltr	and	2 ltr
UK	200	or	50 g	or	250 g	1 ltr	and	2 ltr

Currency restrictions. Tourists may bring an unlimited amount of Spanish or foreign currency into the country and take out up to the equivalent of 500,000 pesetas.

I've nothing to declare.   **No tengo nada que declarar.**
It's for my personal use.   **Es para mi uso personal.**

D

DISABLED TRAVELLERS

There are wheelchair ramps at the major airports, and many larger apartments and hotels do make provision for disabled guests. Some of the more modern resorts also provide ramps to cross pavements. The facilities at Los Cristianos are renowned among disabled travellers and the Marisol Resort in particular specializes in holidays for disabled travellers and their families. In the UK, contact RADAR, 12 City Forum, 250 City Road, London EC1V 8AF (tel. 0171 250 3222).

The streets of large towns such as Santa Cruz de Tenerife and Las Palmas are very difficult to negotiate, due to narrow, high pavements and lack of parking space.

For general information on facilities for disabled travellers in the Canary Islands, contact Federation ECOM, Balmes, 311 Ent. 2, 08006, Barcelona (tel. 217 3882).

DRIVING

Arrival. In the unlikely event that you decide to take your own car to the islands you will need your car registration papers, a nationality plate or sticker, a red warning triangle, a Green Card extension to your regular insurance policy, and a bail bond, which can also be arranged through your insurance company. You will also require an International Driving Permit.

Driving conditions. The rules are the same as in mainland Spain and the rest of the Continent: drive on the right, overtake on the left, yield right of way to all vehicles coming from your right. Speed limits are 120 km/h (74 mph) on motorways, 100 km/h (62 mph) on dual carriageways, and 50 km/h (31 mph) in built-up areas.

Roads vary from six-lane motorway (in Santa Cruz de Tenerife) to primitive tracks (any rural area). In the central areas of Las Palmas (on Gran Canaria) and Santa Cruz and Puerto de la Cruz (on Tenerife), traffic is appalling and one-way systems confusing. Do not drive unless you have to in these towns. Even in provincial towns traffic can be surprisingly heavy and one-way systems are the norm.

Many roads are narrow and twisting, though quite delightful as long as you are not in a hurry. The locals often are, so move over and let them pass, if you can. Always slow down when passing through villages. Be aware that at any time you may suddenly come across a herd of goats, a donkey and cart, a large pothole, or a fall of rocks around the next bend.

Always allow more time than you think a journey will take from simply looking at the map. Driving on mountain roads all day can be very tiring, so take frequent breaks.

Parking. Parking in large towns is very difficult and if your hotel is in a pedestrianized area you may have to park a long way away.

It is an offence to park the car facing against the traffic.

Traffic police. Armed civil guards (Guardia Civil) patrol the roads on black motorcycles. In towns the municipal police handle traffic

Canary Islands

control. If you are fined for a traffic offence you will have to pay on the spot.

Rules and regulations. Always carry your driving licence with you. As the police can demand to see your passport at any time, it is also a good idea to have a photocopy of the important pages of your passport with you.

Spanish law requires that your car should carry a set of spare head-lamp and rear-lamp bulbs. Check this when you are hiring the car.

Motorcyclists and pillion riders must wear crash helmets and motorcycle lights must always be switched on.

Seat belts are compulsory everywhere. Children under the age of ten must travel in the rear.

Fluid measures

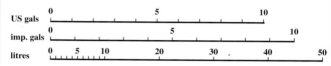

Distance

Breakdowns. Repairs are usually dealt with promptly, due to the large number of repair workshops and skill of their mechanics. Examine tyres and equipment for changing a wheel before hiring a car. It is illegal for a rental company to hire out a car with defective tyres.

Road signs. Aside from the standard pictographs you may encounter the following:

Aparciamento	Parking
Atención	Caution
Blandones	Soft verge
Ceda el paso	Give way

Despacio	Slow
Desprendimientos	Landslide
Desviación	Diversion
Escuela	School
Estacionamiento prohibido	No parking
Obras	Road works
¡Pare!	Stop
Peatones	Pedestrians
Peligro	Danger
Salida de camiones	Lorry exit
carné de conducir	Driving licence
permiso de circulación	Car registration papers
carta verde	Green card
¿Se puede aparcar aqui?	Can I park here?
Llénelo, por favor, con super.	Fill the tank please, top grade.
Por favor, controle el aceite/ los neumáticos/la batería.	Check the oil/tyres/battery.
Mi coche se ha estropeado.	I've had a breakdown.
Ha habido un accidente.	There has been an accident.

E

ELECTRIC CURRENT *(corriente eléctrica)*

Both 110- and 220-volt current may be found, depending on the age of the building. If in doubt, ask.

If you have trouble with an appliance ask the desk clerk at your hotel or your courier to recommend an *electricista*.

What's the voltage – 110 or 220?	**¿Cuál es el voltaje – ciento diez o doscientos veinte?**
an adaptor	**un adaptor**
a battery	**una pila**

EMERGENCIES *(urgencia)*

If your hotel desk clerk isn't available to help, here are some

Canary Islands

emergency numbers:

	Province Santa Cruz de Tenerife	Las Palmas de Gran Canaria
Municipal police	091	091
Civil Guard	062	062
Fire	22 00 80	20 71 22
Hospital	64 10 11	23 11 99

Depending on the nature of the emergency, see also CONSULATES, MEDICAL CARE, POLICE, etc.

ETIQUETTE

Canarians are very easy-going and share with their mainland cousins a belief in the virtues of mañana. Don't try to rush them; far from making things better, it might lengthen the delay. Smile and take your time too.

In a restaurant you must always ask for the bill ("*la cuenta, por favor*"). It is very rarely offered before you ask for it because no waiter wants to be seen to be actually encouraging you to leave.

The Canarians are a very polite people and will always use *por favor* and *gracias*. It is always polite to start a conversation with *Buenos días, Buenos tardes,* or *Buenos noches* (Good morning, good evening, or good night, respectively). A Canarian will usually greet other people on entering a waiting room, small shop, or other such public place.

G

GETTING TO THE CANARY ISLANDS

By air. See also AIRPORTS. There are regular cheap charter flights to the Canaries from Britain and most major cities in Western Europe. Scheduled flights are expensive, infrequent, and usually fly via Madrid.

Flights from the USA usually also go via Madrid, but some airlines offer direct flights in winter.

By ship. Las Palmas on Gran Canaria is no longer a major port of call for cruise liners and only the occasional large passenger ship now calls in.

From the mainland, regular Spanish passenger and mail ships travel from Barcelona or Cadiz to the Canaries. For more information, contact Transmeditter_anea, c/Pedro Muñoz Seca, 2, 28001 Madrid; tel. (34-1) 431-0700; fax. (34-1) 431-0804.

GUIDES and TOURS

All the major islands are comprehensively covered by tour operators, whose coaches take tourists to anywhere and everywhere that is worth seeing, both day and night. Commentaries are given in all major languages, though it never harms to specify at the time of booking the language you require.

If you have a hire car you can, of course, do the vast majority of these things yourself at a fraction of the price (though you may miss certain churches, craft workshops, and demonstrations which open only when coach parties visit).

Boat excursions are another matter and it is well worth taking to the waves in a group, particularly on a whale and dolphin cruise (see page 84). Jeep safaris, where you are driven over potentially dangerous terrain by qualified drivers, are an excellent way of seeing some of the most dramatic island scenery.

Tours can be booked through your hotel reception and most travel agents. If you would like a personal guide to a particular place, the tourist office should be able to direct you to local guides and tell you their rates.

We'd like an English-speaking guide.	**Queremos un guia hable inglés.**

LANGUAGE

The Spanish spoken in the Canary Islands is slightly different from that of the mainland. For instance, islanders don't lisp when they pronounce the letters *c* or *z*. Students of Spanish may detect that the language of the Canaries is spoken with a slight lilt, reminiscent of the Caribbean. Indeed, a number of New World words and expressions are used. The most commonly heard are *guagua* (pronounced

Canary Islands

wah-wah), meaning bus, and *papa*, meaning potato. In tourist areas, German, English, and, to a lesser extent, French are spoken, or at least understood. A large influx of Scandinavian tourists means that you will also hear Swedish and Finnish voices.

Hello (informal)	**Hola**
Good morning/Good day	**Buenos días**
Good afternoon/Good evening	**Buenos tardes**
Good night	**Buenos noches**
Please	**Por favor**
Thank you	**Gracias**
You're welcome	**De nada**
Goodbye	**Adiós**

The Berlitz SPANISH PHRASEBOOK AND DICTIONARY covers most situations you are likely to encounter in your travels in Spain and the Canaries. In addition, the Berlitz Spanish-English/English-Spanish pocket dictionary also contains a menu-reader supplement.

Do you speak English?	**¿Habla usted inglés?**
I don't speak Spanish.	**No hablo español.**

LOST PROPERTY

The first thing to do when you discover you have lost something is obviously to retrace your steps. If you still cannot find the missing item, report the loss to the Municipal Police or the Guardia Civil (see POLICE).

I've lost my wallet/handbag/passport.	**He perdido mi cartera/bolso/pasaporte.**

MAPS

Roads are being built and upgraded continuously on the islands, and yesterday's dirt track is today's highway, which creates a problem for the cartographers. You will probably do better to buy an island map before departure, since maps bought locally are not necessarily the most accurate. Ensure that whichever map you do decide to buy is as up-to-date as possible, then ask your hotel clerk or courier to advise you on your specific route before setting out.

MEDICAL CARE

EC residents should obtain form E111, which entitles them to free medical treatment while on holiday in the Canaries. It is unwise to travel without health insurance as treatment can be expensive.

Many tourists from northern climes suffer painful sunburn through too much exposure on the first day or two. Falling asleep on the beach is a common cause. Take the sun in short doses for at least the first few days. Hangovers can be a problem too, so go steady on the alcohol as well. Spirits are poured in liver-crippling measures and the beer also packs a punch. Drink plenty of bottled mineral water to avoid dehydration.

A list of doctors who speak your language is available at local tourist offices. There are hospitals in all the principal towns and first-aid stations in smaller places.

Chemist's (*farmacia*) are recognizable by a green cross sign and are open during normal shopping hours. After hours, at least one per town remains open all night, the *farmacia de guardia*. Its location is posted in the window of the other *farmacias*.

Where's the nearest (all-night) chemist?	**¿Dónde éstá la farmacia (de guardia) más cercana?**
I need a doctor/dentist.	**Necesito un médico/dentista.**
sunburn	**quemadura del sol**
sunstroke	**una insolación**
a fever	**fiebre**
an upset stomach	**molestias de estómago**
insect bite	**una picadura de insecto**

MONEY MATTERS

Currency. The monetary unit of Spain is the peseta (abbreviated pta).
  Coins: 1, 5, 10, 25, 50, 100, 200, and 500 pesetas.
  Banknotes: 1,000, 2,000, 5,000, and 10,000 pesetas.
  For currency restrictions see CUSTOMS AND ENTRY FORMALITIES.

Banking hours are usually from 9 a.m. to 2 p.m. Monday to Friday and from 9 a.m. to 1 p.m. on Saturdays (except from 1 June to 31

Canary Islands

August when they close on Saturdays), but watch out for all the holidays for which Spain is famous!

Outside normal banking hours, many travel agencies and other businesses displaying a *cambio* sign will change foreign currency into pesetas. All larger hotels will also change guests' money. The exchange rate is slightly less than at the bank. Traveller's cheques always get a better rate than cash. You must take your passport with you when changing money or traveller's cheques.

Credit cards, traveller's cheques, Eurocheques. These are accepted in most hotels, restaurants, and big shops.

Where's the nearest bank/currency exchange office?	**¿Dónde está el banco más cercano/la oficina de cambio más cercana?**
I want to change some pounds/dollars.	**Quiero cambiar libres/dólares.**
Do you accept traveller's cheques?	**¿Acepta usted cheques de viaje?**
Can I pay with this credit card?	**¿Puede pagar con esta tarjeta de crédito?**

PLANNING YOUR BUDGET

The following list will give you some idea of what to expect in the Canaries. As it is impossible to keep up with inflation, however, please consider these as approximations and add a small contingency figure on top.

Apartments. Prices vary widely but here are averages per night for a family apartment: 4 keys, 12,000 ptas and above; 3 keys 6,800–12,000 ptas; 2 keys 4,500–6,800 ptas; 1 key under 4,500 ptas. Discounts are often available for bookings of a week or more.

Attractions. Tenerife: Bananera El Guanche 675 ptas, Loro Parque 1,950 ptas. Gran Canaria: Palmitos Parque 1,900 ptas. Lanzarote: Montañas del Fuego 700 ptas, Jameos del Agua 600 ptas. General: Submarine trips about 3,900 ptas, water parks around 1,500 ptas.

Baby sitters. From 500 ptas per hour.

Bicycle hire. 500 ptas per hour.

Car hire (average of local companies). Group A (Seat Marbella) 1–3 days 2,600 ptas per day; 7 days 16,800 ptas. Group B (Opel Corsa/Renault 5) 1–3 days 3,100 ptas per day; 7 days 18,500 ptas. Group C (Opel Kadett/Ford Fiesta/Ford Escort) 1–3 days 3,500 ptas per day; 7 days 21,000 ptas. Suzuki jeep 1–3 days 6,200 ptas per day; 7 days 40,000 ptas. All prices include third-party insurance only. Comprehensive insurance starts at 1,000 ptas per day on Group A cars, rising to over 2,000 ptas for jeeps.

Excursions (all prices include lunch). Island tour (Gran Canaria, Tenerife) 3,000–4,000 ptas; Jeep safari 4,000 ptas; Gomera day trip from Tenerife 7,500 ptas; boat trips, around 4,000 ptas.

Film. Kodak Gold 24 exp. 500 ptas.

Hotels (double room with bath/shower in high season). 5-star more than 19,000 ptas; 4-star 12,000–19,000 ptas; 3-star 6,500–12,000 ptas; 2-star under 6,500 ptas.

Meals and drinks. Continental breakfast from 500 ptas; *Menú del día* from 800 ptas; three-course lunch/dinner in a fairly good establishment from 1,500 ptas; coffee from 100 ptas; Spanish brandy from 225 ptas; beer (local) from 150 ptas; soft drink from 125 ptas. Prices in luxury hotel bars are much higher.

Motorcycle hire (250cc). 7,500 ptas per day.

Museums. 100–400 ptas, sometimes free.

Nightlife. Casino admission 500 ptas; disco from 600 ptas (includes first drink); cabaret nightclub (including meal) 4,000–5,000 ptas.

Public transport. Buses 75–100 ptas.

Shopping bag. 1 lb (500 g) loaf of bread 80–425 ptas; 1/2 lb (250 g) butter 115 ptas; 6 eggs 90 ptas; 1 lb (500 g) beefsteak 850–950 ptas; 1/2 lb (250 g) local ground coffee from 180 ptas; bottle of wine from 175 ptas (good wine from 400 ptas); 1 3/4 pints (1 litre) fruit juice from 180 ptas.

Sports. Golf: green fee 4–5,000 ptas per day; club hire from 1,000 ptas. Horse-riding from 2,500 ptas. Tennis from 500 ptas per hour.

Canary Islands

Taxis. 30 ptas per kilometre. If you hail a taxi in the street or call one out there is an additional flat charge of 115 ptas.

Water sports. Diving: beginner's course 3,000 ptas; advanced divers, one dive 3,000 ptas. Water skiing (one turn) 2,500 ptas. Jet-skiing (30 mins) 3,000 ptas. Windsurfing 1,300 ptas per hour; 3,500 ptas per day.

NEWSPAPERS and MAGAZINES *(periódico; revista)*

Major British and Continental newspapers are on sale in the Canaries the day after publication. English-language newspapers and magazines that give Canarian news and tourist information include *Here and Now*, a bi-weekly newspaper available from newsagents in Tenerife, *Lanzarote Holiday* magazine, and *Lancelot* magazine, both free from hotels and tourist information offices. German-language newspapers and magazines are also available.

Have you any English-language newspapers?   **¿Tiene periódicos en inglés?**

OPENING HOURS

These vary but generally work around the siesta, with whole towns and villages literally going to sleep during the mid-afternoon.

Banks and Post Offices. 9 a.m. to 2 p.m. Monday to Friday, 9 a.m. to 1 p.m. Saturday (banks are closed on Saturdays from 1 June to 31 August).

Bars and restaurants. It is difficult to generalize, but in the resorts many bars are open from noon or earlier until the small hours. Similarly, informal restaurants will open all day whereas the more up-market establishments will open for lunch and dinner only. Many bars and restaurants are closed one day a week to give their staff a break.

Museums. Variable. Most are open between 10 a.m. and 1 p.m. and re-open from 3 or 4 p.m. to 6 or 7 p.m. Some open on Saturday morning and all day Sunday while others close on Sunday.

Shops. 9 a.m. to 1 p.m. and 4 or 5 p.m. to 7 or 8 p.m. Monday to Saturday.

PHOTOGRAPHY/VIDEO

All popular brands and types of film, camera batteries, flash batteries, and general accessories are sold in the Canaries at competitive prices. For print films, 24-hour processing is widely available. When buying video cassettes, be sure that they will be compatible with your equipment back home.

Field workers and other local people can make very photogenic models but always ask for their permission before you take their picture. Most do not mind and are often quite amused, but some older folk will turn away. Do not harass them.

It is forbidden to take photographs or film videos of any military bases, military or naval port areas, police, government, or military personnel.

I'd like film for this camera.	**Quisiera un carrete para esta máquina.**
a slide film	**un carrete de diapositivas**
a print film	**un carrete para película**

POLICE *(policía)*

There are three police forces in Spain. The best known are the *Guardia Civil* (Civil Guard). Each town also has its own *Policía Municipal* (municipal police), whose uniform varies depending on the town and season but is mostly blue and grey. The third force, the *Cuerpo Nacional de Policía,* a national anti-crime unit, can be recognized by its light brown uniform. All police officers are armed. If you need police assistance you can call on any of these forces. Spanish police are strict but courteous to foreign visitors.

Where is the nearest police station?

¿Dónde está la comisaría más cercana?

POST OFFICES

These are for mail and telegrams, not telephone calls. Stamps *(sellos or timbres)* are sold at any tobacconist's *(tabacos)* and by most shops selling postcards.

Post boxes are painted yellow. If one of the slots is marked *extranjero,* it is for letters abroad.

Poste restante *(general delivery)* If you don't know in advance where you will be staying, you can still have mail forwarded to you, addressed poste restante (lista de correos) at whichever town is most convenient: Ms Jane Smith, Lista de Correos, Puerto de la Cruz, Tenerife, Spain.

When collecting mail you must take your passport to the post office as identification.

Where is the (nearest) post office?

¿Dónde está la oficina de correos (más cercana)?

Have you received any mail for ...?

¿Ha recibido correo para ...?

A stamp for this letter/postcard, please.

Por favor, un sello para esta carta/tarjeta.

PUBLIC HOLIDAYS *(fiesta)*

1 January	**Año Nuevo**	New Year's Day
6 January	**Epifanía**	Epiphany
19 March	**San José**	St Joseph's Day
1 May	**Día del Trabajo**	Labour Day
25 July	**Santiago Apóstol**	St James's Day
15 August	**Asunción**	Assumption
12 October	**Día de la Hispanidad**	Discovery of America Day (Colombus Day)
1 November	**Todos los Santos**	All Saints' Day
25 December	**Navidad**	Christmas Day

In addition to these Spanish national holidays, many purely local and lesser religious, civic, and other holidays are celebrated in various towns of the archipelago (see Festivals, pages 78).

Movable dates:		
	Jueves Santo	Maundy Thursday
	Viernes Santo	Good Friday
	Lunes de Pascua	Easter Monday (Catalonia only)
	Corpus Christi	Corpus Christi
	Inmaculada Concepción	Immaculate Conception (normally 8 December)

PUBLIC TRANSPORT

Bus services. Within the large towns buses run often and are fast and cheap. Tickets are purchased on board and change is given. Buses to other parts of the island still provide a good service but are not designed for tourists. Infrequent timetables and diversions to local villages may therefore make them unsuitable.

Boat services. Boat schedules vary and are published in local papers. There are usually several sailings a day between Tenerife and Gran Canaria. A jetfoil service operates between the two islands, dependent on the weather. There is a daily ferry service between Tenerife (Los Cristianos) and Gomera, and service on Tuesdays, Thursdays, Saturdays, and Sundays from El Hierro to Gomera and daily from Gomera to El Hierro.

Where is the bus stop?	**¿Dónde está la parada de guaguas?**
When is the next bus/boat for ...?	**¿A qué hora sale el próximo guagua/barco para ...?**
I want a ticket to ...	**Quiero un billete para ...**
single (one-way)	**ida**
return (round-trip)	**ida y vuelta**
to get off?	**que bajar?**

R

RADIO and TV *(radio; televisión)*

Most hotels have TV lounges where Canaries TV channels, mostly from the mainland and all in Spanish, can be watched. Tourist hotels also have satellite channels broadcasting several stations in many languages.

Travellers with short-wave radios will be able to pick up the BBC World Service and the Voice of America quite clearly at night and in the early morning. The larger islands all include some English language news and tourist information in their programming. For details pick up an English-language publication (see NEWSPAPERS AND MAGAZINES).

RELIGION

The national religion of Spain is Roman Catholic. Masses are said in almost all churches throughout the islands. In the principal tourist centres Catholic services are also held in foreign languages.

Catholic and Protestant services in various languages are organized regularly in the Ecumenical Temple of Maspalomas on Gran Canaria and at the Catholic church of San Eugenio in Las Américas, Tenerife.

There is an Anglican church in Taoro Park, Puerto de la Cruz, Tenerife, and in the Ciudad Jardín suburb of Las Palmas, Gran Canaria. There is a synagogue in Calle Remedios in Las Palmas and another in Calle Bethencourt, Santa Cruz.

RESTAURANTS

See the chapter on Eating Out and the list of recommended establishments in the centre of this guide. In addition to the recommended list, *Paradors* always serve the very best in local food and, although not cheap, always provide good value. On Lanzarote, any place which César Manrique was once associated with can be relied on for good local food.

T

TAXIS

The letters SP (*servicio publico*) on the front and rear bumpers of a car indicate that it is a taxi. It will probably also have a green light in the front windsreen or a green sign indicating libre when it is available for hire. Taxis are unmetered in tourist areas. There are fixed prices displayed on a board at the main taxi rank, giving the fares to the most popular destinations. These are reasonable. If in doubt, ask the driver before you set off.

Where can I get a taxi?	**¿Dónde puedo coger un taxi?**
What's the fare to ...?	**¿Cuánto es la tarifa a ...?**

TELEPHONES (*teléfono*)

The cheapest and easiest way to make a call, whether local or international, is in a *teléfonico* kiosk. You go to a numbered booth, dial the number yourself, and pay the person at the desk who has metered your call. Alternatively you can now dial internationally from any street-corner telephone. You will need a plentiful supply of change, however, to keep feeding in. Easy-to-follow instructions in all languages are provided with each phone.

If you must call home from your hotel ask in advance how much a three minute-call will cost. It is cheapest after 10 p.m.

Can you get me this number in ...?	**¿Puede communicarme con este número en ...?**
reverse charges	**cobro revertido**

TIME DIFFERENCES

In winter the Canaries maintain Greenwich Mean Time, which is one hour behind most European countries, including Spain. For the rest of the year the islands go on summer time, as does Spain – keeping the one-hour difference.

Canary Islands

Winter time chart

Los Angeles	New York	London	**Canaries**	Madrid
4 a.m.	7 a.m.	noon	**noon**	1 p.m

TIPPING

Since a service charge is normally included in hotel and restáurant bills, tipping is not obligatory. The following are merely suggestions as to what to leave.

Hotel porter, per bag	100 ptas
Maid, per week	200 ptas
Waiter	10%
Taxi driver	10%
Hairdresser	10%
Tourist guide	10% (or around 200 ptas)

TOILETS

The most commonly used expressions for toilets in the Canaries are *servicios* or *aseos*, though you may also hear or see WC, water, and *retretes*.

Public convenences are rare, but all hotels, bars, and restaurants have toilets, usually of a reasonable standard. It is considered polite to buy a coffee if you do drop into a bar just to use the toilet.

Where are the toilets?   **¿Dónde están los servicios?**

TOURIST INFORMATION OFFICES *(oficina de turismo)*

Information on the Canaries may be obtained from Spanish National Tourist Offices, maintained in many countries.

Australia: 203 Castlereagh St, Suite 21a, PO Box A-685, 2000 Sydney NSW; tel: (02) 264 7966.

Canada: 102 Bloor St West, 14th floor, Toronto, Ontario, M5S 1M8; tel. (416) 961 3131/4079.

United Kingdom: 57–58, St James St, London SW1A 1LD; tel (071) 499-0901.

USA: 666 Fifth Ave, New York, NY 10022; tel (212) 265-8822.

8383 Wilshire Blvd, Suite 960, Beverly Hills, CA 90211; tel (213) 658-7188.

1211 Brickell Ave, Miami, FL 33131; tel (305) 358-1992.

During your holiday, information on the islands may be obtained from the following locations. Staff are not always well informed, however, and do not always speak English:

Tenerife: Playa de las Américas, by Pueblo Canario; Puerto de la Cruz, Plaza de la Iglesia; Santa Cruz, Palacio del Cabildo Insular, off Plaza de España.

Gran Canaria: Las Palmas, Casa del Turismo opposite Santa Catalina Park, also Pueblo Canario; Maspalomas, Insular Tourism Centre, corner of Avenida España and Avenida Estados Unidos.

Lanzarote: Parque Municipale, Arrecife.

Fuerteventura: Calle Rosario, Puerto del Rosario.

La Palma: Calle O'Daly, Santa Cruz.

Where is the tourist office?   **¿Dónde está la oficina de turismo?**

W

WATER *(agua)*

Tap water is safe to drink but is not recommended for its taste. The Spaniards almost invariably drink bottled water.

a bottle of sparkling/still   **una botella de agua mineral**
mineral water   **con gas/sin gas**
Is this drinking water   **¿El agua es potable?**

Y

YOUTH HOSTELS

There aren't any in the Canaries. The choice for budget holiday-makers is therefore either to find cheap rooms or to go camping. See CAMPING and following chapter, RECOMMENDED HOTELS.

SOME USEFUL EXPRESSIONS

yes/no	**sí/no**
please/thank you	**por favor/gracias**
excuse me/you're welcome	**perdone/de nada**
where/when/how	**dónde/cuándo/cómo**
how long/how far	**cuánto tiempo/a qué distancia**
yesterday/today/tomorrow	**ayer/hoy/mañana**
day/week/month/year	**dia/semana/mes/ano**
left/right	**izquierda/derecha**
up/down	**arriba/abajo**
good/bad	**bueno/malo**
big/small	**grande/pequeño**
cheap/expensive	**barato/caro**
hot/cold	**caliente/frio**
old/new	**viejo/nuevo**
open/closed	**abierto/cerrado**
here/there	**aqui/alli**
free (vacant)/occupied	**libre/ocupado**
early/late	**temprano/tarde**
easy/difficult	**fácil/dificil**
Does anyone here speak English?	**¿Hay alguien aqui que hable inglés?**
What does this mean?	**¿Qué quiere decir esto?**
I don't understand.	**No comprendo.**
Please write it down.	**Escribamelo, por favor.**
Waiter!/Waitress!	**¡Camarero!/¡Camarera!**
I'd like ...	**Quisiera ...**
How much is that?	**¿Cuánto es?**
Have you something less expensive?	**¿Tiene algo más barato?**
Just a minute.	**Un momento.**
Help me, please.	**Ayudeme, por favor.**
Get a doctor, quickly!	**¡Llamen a un médico, rapidamente!**

A SELECTION
OF HOTELS
AND RESTAURANTS

Recommended Hotels

Below is a selection of hotels in different price bands for each island. Book well in advance, particularly for *paradores* and if visiting the islands in high season or during *Carnaval*. There is a central reservation point for *Paradores* in Madrid. Contact Paradores de España, Central de Reservas, Requana 1, 28013, Madrid (tel. 559 00 69, fax 559 32 33). *Paradores* also have representatives in other countries. In the UK contact Kaytel International (tel. 0171 402 8182 and in the USA contact Marketing Ahead (tel. 212 686 9213). Enquire at the Spanish National Tourist Office in other countries.

The star rating or key rating in brackets after each hotel name refers to the official government grading system (see page 105). As a basic guide to room prices we have used the following symbols (for a double room with bath/shower in high season):

✪	below 7,000 ptas
✪✪	7,000–12,000 ptas
✪✪✪	above 12,000 ptas

TENERIFE

Hotel Mencey (5 stars) ✪✪✪ *Avenida Dr José Naveiras, 38, 380041 Santa Cruz.; Tel. 27 67 00, fax 28 00 17.* Probably the finest hotel on the islands and on a par with the world's great hotels. Patios and balconies, antiques, and art. 293 rooms.

Hotel Meliá San Felipe (4 stars) ✪✪✪
Avenida Marqués Villanueva del Prado, Puerto de la Cruz; Tel. 38 40 11, fax 38 65 59. Guests have a view of the sea or Mount Teide at this beachfront resort hotel. Olympic size pool and floodlit tennis. 260 rooms.

Hotel Monopol (3 stars) ✪✪ *Quintana, 15, 38400, Puerto de la Cruz; Tel. 38 46 11; fax 37 03 10.* A charming family-run establishment in the centre of town, famous for its Canarian balconies and its tropical-style patio. Simple modern facilities plus roof-top pool. 92 rooms.

Parador de Cañadas del Teide (2 stars) ✪✪ *Cañadas del Teide, 38300, La Orotava.; Tel./fax 38 64 15.* This chalet-style *Parador* has a superb setting in the foothills of Mount Teide next to Los Roques. Rustic furnishings. 23 rooms.

Hotel Jardín Tropical del Teide (4 stars) ✪✪✪ *Urbanización San Eugenio, 38660 Playa de las Américas; Tel. 79 41 11; fax 79 44 51.* This Moorish fantasy is probably the most beautiful building on the south coast. Beautiful gardens, lovely decor. 380 rooms.

Pueblo Torviscas Apartments (3 keys) ✪✪ *Urb. Torviscas, Adeje; Tel. 75 07 50.* Only a short walk from the beach, these attractive studios enjoy a lovely garden setting, backed by mountain scenery. Very popular. 50 apartments.

GRAN CANARIA

Hotel Reina Isabel (5 stars) ✪✪✪ *35008 Las Palmas. Tel. 26 01 00; fax 27 45 58.* The capital's most luxurious hotel with excellent restaurant, roof-top pool and nightclub. 233 rooms.

Hotel Santa Catalina (5 stars) ✪✪✪ *Parque Doramas, León y Castillo, 277, 35005 Las Palmas; Tel. 24 30 40, fax 24 27 64.* This historic building has been used by both British and Spanish royalty and enjoys a splendid leafy position. 206 rooms.

Club de Mar (2 keys) ✪ *Playa de Mogán, 35140, Puerto Mogán; Tel. 56 50 66, fax 74 02 23.* Situated in the mini-village of hotels and apartments around the beautiful marina of Puerto Mogán and designed to blend in with the local town-house style. 160 rooms.

Canary Islands

Aparthotel Escorial (2 stars) ✪✪ *Avenida de Italia, 6, Playa del Inglés; Tel. 76 13 58.* Attractively furnished apartments close to the busy centre and a ten-minute walk from the beach. 251 apartments.

LANZAROTE

Hotel Los Fariones (4 stars) ✪✪✪ *Roque del Este, 1 35510 Puerto del Carmen.; Tel. 51 01 75; fax 51 02 02.* Long-established hotel sited on a fine beach with virtually its own secluded cove and a luxurious palm garden in its grounds. Quiet atmosphere, central location. 242 rooms.

Apartamentos Lanzamar (3 keys) ✪✪ *Calle Guardilama, Puerto del Carmen; Tel 51 00 08; fax 51 09 04.* Ideal quiet location set back a few streets above the beach and a five-minute walk from the old town. Well-equipped rooms and attractive pool. 112 apartments.

Apartments Tahiche (3 keys) ✪✪ *Plaza Montaña Clara, Costa Teguise; Tel. 59 01 17.* Attractive three-storey complex in green and white local architectural style, near both beach and resort centre. 238 apartments.

Playa Flamingo Apartments (2 keys) ✪✪ *Urbanización Montaña Roja, Playa Blanca, 35570 Yaiza; Tel. 51 73 69.* These attractive, low-level apartments enjoy a fine beachside setting. Exteriors are whitewashed, Moorish-style; interiors are modern with stripey fabrics and pine. 305 apartments.

FUERTEVENTURA

Hotel Riu Palace Tres Islas (5 stars) ✪✪✪ *Playa Corralejo, 35660 Corralejop; Tel. 53 57 00; fax 53 58 58.* A modern seven-storey block perfectly located on the magnificent beach with a view of the dunes. Attractive pool and terrace, every facility. 365 rooms.

Apartamentos Corralejo Beach (3 keys) ✪ *Avenida del Generalisimo Franco, Corralejo; Tel. 86 63 15–18.* Excellent studios sited in the port area, 3 miles (5 km) from the famous beach, but very handy for town and night life. 158 apartments.

Bungalows Castillo Playa (2 keys) ✪ *Castillo Playa, Caleta de Fuste; Tel. 85 04 24.* A small cluster of 80 local-style bungalows around a pool and garden area; part of a larger complex with all facilities, near the beach.

GOMERA

Conde de la Gomera Parador (4 stars) ✪✪✪ *Balcón de la Villa y Puerto Apartado, 21, San Sebastián; Tel. 87 11 00; fax 87 11 16.* One of the finest examples of a *parador*, this comfortable country manor is beautifully furnished and has a superb cliff-top site. 58 rooms.

Hotel Jardín Tecina (3 stars) ✪✪ *Lomada de Tecina, 38810 Playa de Santiago; Tel. 89 50 50; fax 89 51 88.* This stylish traditionally designed, low-rise complex owned by shipping magnate Fred Olsen effectively forms the only resort on the island. All facilities. 434 rooms.

LA PALMA

Parador Santa Cruz de la Palma (3 stars) ✪✪ *Avenida Marítíma, 34, Santa Cruz de la Palma; Tel. 41 23 40; fax 41 18 56.* A modest but attractive parador which blends almost unnoticed into the weather-beaten balconied buildings lining the seafront. 32 rooms.

EL HIERRO

Parador El Hierro (3 stars) ✪✪✪ *Las Playas, El Hierro; Tel. 55 80 36; fax 55 80 86.* This secluded 20-year-old building is perfect for getting away from it all. Facilities include swimming pool. 47 rooms.

Recommended Restaurants

We appreciated the food and service in the restaurants listed below; if you find other places that you think are worth recommending we'd be pleased to hear from you.

To give you an idea of price (for a three-course meal per person, including half a bottle of house wine), we have used the following symbols:

✪	under 1,500 ptas
✪✪	1,500–2,500 ptas
✪✪✪	over 2,500 ptas

TENERIFE

La Isla Fisch-Fiete ✪✪ *Calle de Esquivel, 6, Puerto de la Cruz; Tel. 38 00 02.* One of the longest-established restaurants in Puerto, serving local fish and imported specialities.

Mario ✪✪ *Edificio Rincón del Puerto, Plaza del Charco, Puerto de la Cruz; Tel. 38 55 35.* Small fish restaurant with lots of nautical memorabilia. You can even sit in a boat to eat your paella. Closed Mondays.

Mi Vaca y Yo ✪✪✪ *Calle Cruz Verde, 3, Puerto de la Cruz; Tel. 38 52 47.* Superb international food in an exotic sub-tropical setting. A great favourite with tourists. Evenings only.

La Rueda ✪✪ *Carretera General del Norte, Sauzal, near Puerto de la Cru;. Tel. 56 29 81.* Barbecued meats are the speciality at this rustic establishment. Closed Wednesdays.

El Sol ✪✪✪ *Los Cristiano;. Tel. 79 05 69.* Classic French cuisine is the speciality of the house. Highly recommended.

Fortuna ✪✪ *Calle Juan XXIII, Edificio Marcos, Los Cristianos; Tel. 79 17 14.* The extrovert Czech owner here has a loyal following, particularly families, who relish his first-class international and mid-European cuisine. Closed Tuesdays.

Toni's ✪✪✪ *Alcalá, near Puerto de Santiago; Tel. 86 74 27.* Highly acclaimed international restaurant with an island-wide following.

El Dornajo ✪ *Avenida Litoral, Playa de las América;. Tel. 79 14 25.* Típico whose chef/owner serves large portions. Very good value.

GRAN CANARIA

El Cerdo Que Rie ✪✪ *Paseo de las Canteras, 31, Las Palmas.* Excellent international and Spanish food in informal colonial-style surroundings; fondues and flambés are the specialities of "The Laughing Pig."

Dedo de Dios ✪✪ *The harbour, Puerto de las Nieves; Tel. 89 80 00.* Marvellous views of the fishing beach and the rock stack Dedo de Dios (Finger of God). Excellent fish, good salads.

Parador de Cruz de Tejeda ✪✪✪ *Cruz de Tejeda; Tel. 65 80 50.* Set amid beautiful mountain scenery, the Parador (no accommodation) serves the very best in Canarian cooking.

San Agustín Beach Club ✪✪✪✪ *Playa de los Cocoteros, San Agustín; Tel. 76 04 00.* Fine international food plus the very best shellfish is served in generous portions either by the poolside or inside the large, elegant dining room.

LANZAROTE

La Sardina Flamenca ✪✪ *Centro Comercial Montaña Tropical, Calle Toscon, Puerto del Carmen.* This attractive modern restaurant offers the very best grilled fish, shellfish, and meats, accompanied by excellent flamenco dancing. Open every day.

Barito Tapas Bar ✪ *Avenida de Las Playas, Puerto del Carmen.* Small, lively, authentic tapas bar where locals and holidaymakers literally rub shoulders.

Canary Islands

Jardín de Cactus ✪ *Guatiza; Tel. 52 93 97.* Good, simple Canarian lunches are served on a peaceful terrace shaded by an awning overlooking the beautiful gardens. Lunch only. Open every day.

La Era ✪✪ *Yaiza; Tel. 83 00 16.* This charming Canarian tipico has a white-washed courtyard decked with flowers that opens on to two tiny rustic dining rooms, serving outstanding island specialities.

Montañas del Fuego Restaurante ✪✪ *Montañas del Fuego, Parque Nacional de Timanfaya; Tel. 84 00 57.* The food is cooked over the heat of the volcano. Order grilled food and watch it cook. Views over the lava fields. Open every day.

FUERTEVENTURA

La Molina ✪✪ *Antigua.* Canarian specialities are served in the atmospheric outbuildings next to the windmill that gives this restaurant its name.

GOMERA

Las Rosas Restaurant ✪✪ *Carretera General, Las Rosas; Tel. 80 09 16.* Panoramic views and good, solid Canarian food. When coach parties arrive, demonstrations of el silbo, the island's whistling language, are given.

Parador Conde de La Gomera ✪✪✪ *Balcón de la Ville y Puerto Apartado, 21, San Sebastián; Tel. 87 11 00.* Excellent Canarian food in colonial-style surroundings.

LA PALMA

Parador de Santa Cruz ✪✪ *Avenida Marítima, Santa Cruz;. Tel. 41 23 40.* Fine Canarian food in authentic surroundings.

EL HIERRO

Mirador de la Peña ✪✪ *Guarazoca;. Tel. 55 03 00.* Another *mirador* restaurant to benefit from the Manrique treatment. Island specialities are served in a tranquil, modern room with wonderful views.
